Based on the (actual) diary of an anonymous girl

go ask alice

A Full Length Play

by

FRANK SHIRAS

THE DRAMATIC PUBLISHING COMPANY

*** NOTICE ***

The amateur and stock acting rights to this work are controlled exclusively by THE DRAMATIC PUBLISHING COMPANY without whose permission in writing no performance of it may be given. Royalty fees are given in our current catalogue and are subject to change without notice. Royalty must be paid every time a play is performed whether or not it is presented for profit and whether or not admission is charged. A play is performed anytime it is acted before an audience. All inquiries concerning amateur and stock rights should be addressed to:

DRAMATIC PUBLISHING
P. O. Box 129, Woodstock, Illinois 60098.

COPYRIGHT LAW GIVES THE AUTHOR OR THE AUTHOR'S AGENT THE EXCLUSIVE RIGHT TO MAKE COPIES. This law provides authors with a fair return for their creative efforts. Authors earn their living from the royalties they receive from book sales and from the performance of their work. Conscientious observance of copyright law is not only ethical, it encourages authors to continue their creative work. This work is fully protected by copyright. No alterations, deletions or substitutions may be made in the work without the prior written consent of the publisher. No part of this work may be reproduced or transmitted in any form or by any means, electronic or mechanical, including photocopy, recording, videotape, film, or any information storage and retrieval system, without permission in writing from the publisher. It may not be performed either by professionals or amateurs without payment of royalty. All rights, including but not limited to the professional, motion picture, radio, television, videotape, foreign language, tabloid, recitation, lecturing, publication, and reading are reserved. *On all programs this notice should appear:*

"Produced by special arrangement with
THE DRAMATIC PUBLISHING COMPANY of Woodstock, Illinois"

©MCMLXXVI by
PRENTICE-HALL, INC.

Based upon the work "Go Ask Alice"
©MCMLXXI by
PRENTICE-HALL, INC.

Printed in the United States of America
All Rights Reserved
(GO ASK ALICE)

ISBN 0-87129-490-7

GO ASK ALICE
A Full-length Play
For Eight Men and Fifteen Women

CHARACTERS

ALICE ABERDEEN	*sixteen*
HELEN ABERDEEN	*her mother, thirties*
DOUGLAS ABERDEEN	*her father, thirties*
ALEXANDRIA	*her sister, twelve*
TIM	*her brother, fourteen*
BETH	*teen*
SAMUEL	*teen*
CHRIS VETRANO	*her best friend*
JILL PETERS	*teen*
BILL THOMPSON	*teen*
JAN FUJARA	*teen*
JOE DRIGGS	*teen*
GLORIA	*teen*
FREDDIE	*girl teen*
PEG	*teen*
SHEILA	*thirties*
GEORGE	*teen*
JOEL REEMS	*teen*
MARGE	*teen*
GERTRUDE	*twenties*
BABBIE	*teen*
TOM	*teen*
DOCTOR MILLER	*woman psychiatrist, thirties*

The action is in the present and occurs chiefly during Alice Aberdeen's sixteenth year.

ACT ONE
Scene One

LIGHTS: ALICE is amazed that beneath the pounds
   she recently lost there existed a very pleasing
   figure. Growing up eager to meet the world,
   she has repeatedly felt rebuffed, is now dis-
   trustful, although not despairing. ALICE,
   dressed in jeans, is alone, sitting on the bed in
   her room, taking the lock off of a strongbox
   from which she removes her diary. She then
   takes out a handful of pens and pencils, picking
   each up successively and speaking to it.)

ALICE. There you are, you're one of my main men.
   (Another.) You're my most happy fella.
   (Another.) You're a big brute but I love you
   just the same. (Another.) You may be skinny,
   dear friend, but you're ever faithful and I'll
   always, always treasure you. (Another.) And
   you, do you know who you are? You're my
   knight in shining armor, and that's why I'm
   going to write with *you* today. You keep the
   knaves from breaching the moat and capturing
   me. They want to carry me off to their mountain
   hideout but *you* won't let them, and I love you
   for it. (ALICE kisses pen. Knock at door.)
   Who is it?
ALEXANDRIA (offstage). Me!
ALICE. Come in, "me!"

(Enter ALEXANDRIA.)

ALEXANDRIA. Alice, can I borrow your old radio?
ALICE. What for?
ALEXANDRIA. What do you care? It doesn't work good.
ALICE. Okay, Alex, borrow it. It's in my box.
ALEXANDRIA. Why do you keep that old baby box?
ALICE (archly). I have kept it because we are poor and can't afford to buy me a new one.
ALEXANDRIA. We've got enough money, Alice.
ALICE. Take the radio and go.
ALEXANDRIA. Are you gonna write in your diary now?
ALICE. I may.
ALEXANDRIA. What do you write in it? Lies?
ALICE. Alexandria, you're not a brat sister, so stop trying so hard to act like one.
ALEXANDRIA. How come you're so skinny now? You were fat a couple of months ago.
ALICE. I'm not skinny and I was never fat.
ALEXANDRIA. Are you trying to get a boy friend?
ALICE (smiling). I don't like boys.
ALEXANDRIA. I don't either. Tim says you're trying to get a boy friend. Tim says ——
ALICE. You shouldn't listen so much to Timothy. He's just using you to bug his big sister.
ALEXANDRIA. Tim says boys are flies and you're trying to turn into a honey pot. (Laughing, ALICE chases ALEXANDRIA, catches her.) I'm sorry, Alice!
ALICE. You are not. Take the radio and go. (ALEXANDRIA opens box, removes radio.) And be careful of it, Alex. I don't care if it doesn't work well.
ALEXANDRIA (doing salaam). Yes, your

Act I   GO ASK ALICE   Page 7

    worshipful. I don't know why you're worried about this old radio, you just got a new stereo.
ALICE. I like old things. Now, please go so I can write my lies.

(ALEXANDRIA exits. ALICE puts on headphones and begins to write in her diary. She only gets a sentence or two down before her mother, HELEN ABERDEEN, knocks on door. She is in her early thirties, several inches taller than ALICE, slender. Headphones prevent ALICE from hearing knock. MOTHER enters.)

MOTHER. Oh, sorry, I can come back later.
ALICE (removing headphones). Hi, Mom, what did you say?
MOTHER. I'm leaving.
ALICE (laughing). So soon? You're not interrupting me. What do you want?
MOTHER (picking magazine off floor). I forgot what time you said Beth and her friend were coming to watch television with you.
ALICE. In a little while, at nine o'clock.
MOTHER. Who's her friend?
ALICE. I don't know. Some boy.
MOTHER. Oh? That's nice. I'm sure any friend of Beth's is a nice person.
ALICE. He's probably a clod.
MOTHER. Alice, you have a tendency to be cynical, to find fault in ––
ALICE. "If you can't say something nice, don't say anything at all."
MOTHER. I know I repeat that statement, but that doesn't make it any less true.
ALICE. I try to be positive, Mom.

MOTHER. Do you? How hard?

ALICE. Real hard. I smile, I put up my hair, I go out the door and act friendly and show spirit but it doesn't work.

MOTHER. Did you hear yourself? You said you "act" friendly. You have to *be* friendly.

ALICE. I have a friendly mother, a friendly father, a friendly sister and brother — and there's me, a mean little animal who sits in a dark room and growls.

MOTHER. If you feel mean it's only because of your attitude. Your attitude ——

ALICE. —— "determines your altitude."

MOTHER. Do I repeat myself *that* much? But it's true, when you're optimistic, you rise above day-to-day problems and ——

ALICE. Mom, please don't pick up after me.

MOTHER. If you didn't let that fall there, no one would have to pick it up.

ALICE. And please don't dust. Please, Mother, sit down with me.

MOTHER. Look, I'm picking up and dusting because it *needs* it.

ALICE. But can't you sit and talk sometimes for a minute?

MOTHER. You act like I never talk with you. Alice, that isn't true at all.

ALICE. I know it's not. You talk to me.

MOTHER. Well . . .

ALICE. I love you.

MOTHER. But . . . Alice, what's going on? What's the matter?

ALICE. Nothing's the matter. I'm sorry I said I love you. (MOTHER sits, puts arms around ALICE.)

Act I   GO ASK ALICE   Page 9

MOTHER. Now wait a minute. (Cheerily.) Somehow I walked in here and put you in a bad mood. It means a lot to me that you love me. You know that, don't you?

ALICE (noncommitally). Yes, I know it.

MOTHER. Good. You have the whole summer ahead of you. Be positive. Think of all the new friends you're going to make.

ALICE. I'm not so sure I want to make any friends.

MOTHER. What?

ALICE. Kids are stupid. Sometimes I think all us kids are trying to be shadows of each other. We're trying to buy the same records and everything even if we don't like them.

MOTHER. There you go, concentrating on the negative.

ALICE. We're like robots. Off an assembly line.

MOTHER. Now, wait a minute. Your generation is showing signs of being very innovative, very ––

ALICE. Talk about negative! Who can be more negative than *my* generation! We sneer at everything!

MOTHER. Alice! Children your age should ––

ALICE. There, you see. You called me a child again.

MOTHER. Well, you're not an adult.

ALICE. I'm almost sixteen years old, Mother. Don't forget, you were only eighteen when I was born.

MOTHER. That was different.

ALICE. Different? When you're losing an argument, you just say something is different and get out of it that way.

MOTHER. It was different. Both your father and I came from working-class families. In high school he suddenly decided on an academic career. We loved each other very much and got married and I helped put him through the university all the way to his doctorate.

ALICE. You put him through school?

MOTHER. I don't know why I didn't tell you before. It's no secret.

ALICE. That means you had me when you were *poor.*

MOTHER. Alice, are you implying we couldn't afford you?

ALICE. It sounds like you couldn't.

MOTHER. And so didn't *want* you? Is that what you're saying? We *wanted* you.

ALICE. My being born didn't help the situation.

MOTHER. Alice! What's the *matter* with you?

ALICE (crying). I don't know. I don't know what's the matter with me. (MOTHER holds ALICE in her arms, comforts her.)

MOTHER. Now, now. I think you lost weight too fast. You've been starving yourself and getting run down. Now, now. I love you, Alice.

ALICE. Do you really?

MOTHER. Of course I do. I love you very, very much.

ALICE. You never say so. I have to drag it out of you.

MOTHER. I'm sorry. I'll try to say it more. It seems I'm always so busy.

ALICE. I make you work. I leave stuff all over. I'll stop, I promise.

TIM (offstage). Mom! Mom!

MOTHER. I'm in Alice's room! That boy is going to walk right on my waxed kitchen floor!

Act I   GO ASK ALICE   Page 11

(Enter TIM.)

TIM. I didn't walk on your waxed kitchen floor.
MOTHER. No one said you did.
TIM. You were thinking it.
MOTHER. You blame me?
TIM. Mom, guess what?
MOTHER. The Atomic Energy Commission just made you an offer.
TIM. Come on, don't make fun. At the science club meeting I got the word that my exhibit won first prize this summer. (MOTHER and TIM see ALICE put headphones back on, assume she can't hear.)
MOTHER. Really? That's wonderful! I know how hard you worked on that exhibit all year. But then, you *are* an A student. (Adjusting headphones, ALICE overhears.)
TIM. How come Alice only gets C's?
MOTHER. Why this sudden interest in your sister's academic record?
TIM. I don't like it when Alice calls me dumb.
MOTHER. If you hadn't made fun of her plumpness, I'm sure she would never have said anything unpleasant to you. (Doorbell rings.) I'll get it. Alice is expecting company.
TIM. I'm going to my room.
MOTHER. See if you can't do a little positive thinking in there.
TIM. I'll work on it. (Exit MOTHER and TIM. ALICE kicks a pillow on floor; locks up diary.)

(MOTHER reenters with guests. BETH is plump, SAMUEL flabby. Although totally insincere, Samuel's facade takes in most adults.)

MOTHER. Beth, it's nice to see you again. And I'm pleased to meet *you,* Samuel. What program are you going to watch?
SAMUEL. Whatever program Alice wishes, I'm sure. Wouldn't you say so, Beth?
BETH. Yeah.
MOTHER. But you're the guests, you decide.
SAMUEL. In that case I'll consult the television guide, Mrs. Aberdeen.
ALICE. Hi, Beth.
BETH. Hi. This is Samuel.
ALICE. Hello, Samuel.
SAMUEL. Hello, Miss Aberdeen.
MOTHER. Alice.
SAMUEL. Of course. Alice.
MOTHER. Well, you three enjoy television. (Exit MOTHER.)
BETH. I'm gonna use your washroom, Alice. (Exit BETH.)
SAMUEL. Just call me Sammy.
ALICE. Okay, Sammy.
SAMUEL. I like you.
ALICE. You what?
SAMUEL (advancing). I think you're pretty.
ALICE. Hey! Are you for real?
SAMUEL. Do you like me?
ALICE. I think you're marvelous. Stay back so I can marvel from a distance.
SAMUEL. I like you a lot. I wanna kiss you.
ALICE. What were you hatched from?
SAMUEL. Come on, Beth'll be out in a minute.
ALICE. Sammy, were you starved for affection

Act I   GO ASK ALICE   Page 13

    as a baby?
SAMUEL. All you girls just wanna talk. I like
    action.
ALICE. What was that Mr. Goodbar routine you
    were giving my mother?
SAMUEL. You're just stalling around.
ALICE. What program should we watch?
SAMUEL. I've got money. I can send out for a
    pizza.
ALICE. That's nice.
SAMUEL. If you gimme some action.
ALICE. I get a pizza if I give you a kiss?
SAMUEL. A kiss is a start. I'm dynamite. Try
    me, you'll want more than a kiss.
ALICE. Sammy, sit down. Thank you. Sammy,
    you're crazy but I can help you.
SAMUEL (chortling). Touch me. That's all the
    help I need.
ALICE. I'll hit you over the head.
SAMUEL. Why do you girls stall around all the
    time?
ALICE. We like boys who show patience and tact.
SAMUEL. I've got a lot of patience. But all it
    ever gets me is a good-night peck at the door.
ALICE. You're not going to solve your problem
    with force.
SAMUEL. Yes I am!

(SAMUEL charges ALICE, grabs her, tries to kiss
    her as BETH enters.)

ALICE. Stop it!
BETH. You heard her, stop it!
SAMUEL. You sure finished in a hurry.
BETH. I had a quick shower. I'm surprised at you.

Alice is my best friend.
SAMUEL. I should make out with your enemies?
ALICE. Where did you find him, Beth?
BETH. Our parents are friends. (Glares at SAMUEL.) It must be those high-pro kennel rations Sammy's getting now.
SAMUEL. You're not funny, Beth.
BETH. You're not staying here another minute if you don't apologize to Alice.
SAMUEL. I'm sorry, Alice.
ALICE. Okay.
SAMUEL. I'm sorry I didn't get any farther.
BETH. Samuel!
SAMUEL. Okay, okay. Don't yell at *me,* yell at my hormones, they make me do it.
BETH. You don't have any hormones.
SAMUEL. Shut up.
ALICE. Well, now that we're all *friends,* what program should we put on?
SAMUEL. I don't wanna watch TV, lemme put on your headphones.
ALICE. Go ahead. (SAMUEL puts on headphones, ALICE and BETH sit and talk.)
BETH. I'm sorry he's so gross. I'd heard a few stories about him, but I didn't think that ——
ALICE. I understand.
BETH. He's transportation for me. He borrowed his father's car.
ALICE. Beth, you don't have to *apologize.* It's all right.
SAMUEL (taking off headphones). You got anything to eat?
ALICE. I'm waiting for the pizza.
SAMUEL. You didn't earn it.
BETH. There's a bone in my purse, Sammy.

Act I   GO ASK ALICE   Page 15

SAMUEL. Gnaw on it yourself. (Puts headphones back on.)
BETH. This is the last time we see each other.
ALICE. Only for six weeks.
BETH. I guess so. I bet I hate summer camp.
ALICE. No, you won't. Just think of this burg.
BETH. What'll you do all summer?
ALICE. Read books. What else?
BETH. I thought *I* read a lot. You read so many I think you breathe them in. How do you do it?
ALICE. I'm used to it. I was in the hospital a long time when I was eleven from an automobile accident. I started reading then and never stopped, I guess.
BETH. What's that you're reading now?
ALICE. *Madame Bovary.*
BETH. I've heard of it. Isn't it a classic? Something they read in college?
ALICE. I guess so. But it's easy to read. Flaubert — he's the author — was a stylist who tried to write simply. Sometimes he sat in his window all day trying to think of a *single* word and screaming when he couldn't think of it.
BETH. Honest? How do you know?
ALICE. I did a term paper on him for my English class for extra credit to raise my grade.
BETH. What's *Madame Bovary* about?
ALICE. It's this unhappy woman who doesn't have any real friends or lovers, or something, in this place she doesn't like. I hear it has a terrible ending. She swallows something awful.
BETH. Don't tell me, I might read it some day.
ALICE. How can I tell you? I don't know the ending myself.

BETH. I hope there are some decent boys at camp. It'd be just my luck to have someone like Sammy get interested in me.
SAMUEL (removing headphones). What about me?
BETH. What? What? Who said anything about *you?*
SAMUEL. I saw you look my way like you smelled something bad.
BETH. Sammy, you're paranoid.
SAMUEL. What about me? Huh?
ALICE. She only said how you seem to enjoy what you're listening to.
SAMUEL. I've got my favorite rock station on. Want to make something out of it? (Puts headphones back on.)
BETH. You know who I ran into today? Jill Rogers.
ALICE. Jill Rogers? Really? Miss Highest Echelon herself?
BETH. I could never figure out whether she's cool or stuck up.
ALICE. Belonging to the inner core of the inner circle, I think she's stuck up.
BETH. I think she's shallow.
ALICE. She's definitely superficial.
BETH. Really shallow. She never thinks about important things, about values ——
ALICE. She's all glitz. There's more to life than parties and getting a tan at the beach. What happened with Jill?
BETH. She said she was going to call you.
ALICE (excited). Me? Why would she call me?
BETH. Probably about something superficial.
ALICE. Come on, come on. What does she want?
BETH. She acted really friendly. But between you

and me, she wants to be admitted to your dad's university, and is trying to get an inside track.

ALICE. You think so?

BETH. Definitely. I thought I better warn you.

ALICE. Thanks. When did she say she was gonna call?

BETH. Some time this evening, I think. She mentioned something about a party.

ALICE. A *party?*

BETH. I'm glad I got to you before she did.

ALICE. I am, too. If that girl thinks she can use me to work on my father, she's got another think coming.

BETH. Right.

SAMUEL (removing headphones). I wanna go.

BETH. But we just got here.

SAMUEL. I want some action. The night is young. I'm gonna take you home, Beth, then cruise in my dad's car.

BETH. Cruise for what?

SAMUEL. You know.

BETH. It's impolite to leave right after you come.

SAMUEL. You said Alice'd give me some action.

BETH. I what?

SAMUEL. You did, too.

BETH (winking at ALICE). I said, "If it's action you're looking for, Alice'll give you all you want and maybe more."

ALICE. That's right. Whenever you're ready you can have a swift kick.

SAMUEL. Shut up. I'm going.

FATHER (offstage, knocking at door). Alice!

(SAMUEL opens door. FATHER enters.)

SAMUEL. Nice to meet you, sir. I have to be going.
FATHER. You do? Well, but ——
BETH. This is Samuel, my friend. We were visiting Alice.
FATHER. Fine, fine. I'm sorry to interrupt. Nice to see you, Beth.
SAMUEL. You didn't interrupt, sir. Like I said, we were on the way out.
FATHER. Oh, well, in that case, I'll see you to the front door.
ALICE. I'll do that, Dad.
BETH. Don't either of you bother. I know the way out.
ALICE. Well . . .
BETH. 'Bye. Have a good summer.
SAMUEL (closing door). I'm gonna have a lousy one. (BETH and SAMUEL exit.)
FATHER. I just thought I'd look in, Alice. (ALICE makes room for FATHER on bed.) You're so much thinner now. I can't get over it. You're so pretty. Not that you weren't always pretty.
ALICE (unbelieving). Am I pretty, Dad? Really?
FATHER. Of course you are. I'm sure it took a lot of will power to lose that much weight. I'm proud of you — I mean, not because of the weight so much but because of the will power.
ALICE. More than twelve globby pounds of lumpy lard. Mom thinks I overdid it, that I lost it too fast.
FATHER. Do *you* feel all right? That's what's important.
ALICE. I'm kind of nervous lately. I'm having

trouble sleeping. I wish I could sleep. Maybe Mom is right that I dieted too much.

FATHER. That's possible, I guess.

ALICE. Dad, I'm sorry about the C's all year.

FATHER. Hey, what is this?

ALICE. You're a professor. It's awful to have a daughter who's a mental blob.

FATHER. Now hold it right there.

ALICE (taking Father's hand). I'm sorry. I'll try harder. I'll try to overcome my lack of brains with hard work.

FATHER. You don't have any lack of brains.

ALICE. Then why don't I get better grades?

FATHER. As I said before, it's probably the way you apply yourself.

ALICE. I use all those study habits you showed me.

FATHER. Or, as I *also* said, other things may be bothering you and interfering with your concentration.

ALICE (fondling his hand). I don't want to let you down.

FATHER. You're not letting me down.

ALICE. I bet the other profs at the university brag about their kids. "My son who's going to be a doctor." "My daughter, who's brilliant at music theory." Then Professor Aberdeen says, "My daughter, who's a dummy."

FATHER. Please, Alice, it hurts to hear you go on like that.

ALICE. Do you love me?

FATHER. Of course I love you.

ALICE (kissing his hand). Even though I'm not perfect?

FATHER. Especially since you're not perfect. Here, I brought you something.

ALICE. What? Chocolate-covered peanuts! My favorite! But, Daddy, you know I'm on a diet.
FATHER. Cheat a little. Be a little imperfect.
ALICE. I'll only eat six. Six wonderful, delicious, mouth-watering, delectable, heavenly chocolate-covered peanuts. (FATHER chuckles, eats some with ALICE.) Are you sure my grades don't bother you? I mean, a person can't go to college with C's. How would it look for a professor's daughter who can't get accepted at a college?
FATHER. We'll face that when the time comes. Why are you wrinkling up your forehead?
ALICE. I'm sending ESP signals to the telephone, to make it ring.
FATHER. Who's supposed to call?
ALICE. A certain superficial person.
FATHER. Oh. How do you like the stereo?
ALICE. It's wonderful, Daddy. I listen to it all the time. At night when I can't sleep, I put the headphones on and listen to music.
FATHER. You've been having sleeping problems for a while now.
ALICE. A couple of months.
FATHER. Maybe we should have you see the doctor.

(MOTHER enters. The telephone rings.)

ALICE. I'll get it! (ALICE flies from the room, almost bumps into MOTHER. Offstage, into telephone.) Oh, hello, Jill . . . Yes, I *think* Beth mentioned that you might call. How are you? (As FATHER and MOTHER speak, Alice's voice becomes a murmur in background.)
FATHER. You're right, she's upset. She's been

Act I   GO ASK ALICE   Page 21

    trying to become a new person all at once.
MOTHER (getting Alice's nightgown). She needs
    rest. It's not too early to go to bed.
FATHER. She doesn't sleep.
MOTHER. How can a teen-ager have insomnia?
FATHER. Helen, I'm going to give her a sleeping
    pill.
MOTHER. But ——
FATHER. Just tonight.
MOTHER. But that's a prescription drug.
FATHER. It won't hurt her. It's just for tonight.
    If she keeps on having trouble sleeping, I'll
    have her see a doctor.
MOTHER. Well, all right. (FATHER exits to
    Alice's bathroom.)
ALICE (offstage). Good-bye, Jill. It sounds like
    fun.

(ALICE enters.)

MOTHER. Who was that?
ALICE. Jill Peters.
MOTHER. *The* Jill Peters? The Miss Everything?
ALICE. The same.
MOTHER. What did she want?
ALICE. For me to go to a party. This weekend!
    In three days already!
MOTHER. She invited you?
ALICE. How else could I go?
MOTHER. Well, well, well.

(Enter FATHER with red bottle.)

FATHER. Here, Alice, take this. It'll help you
    sleep tonight.

ALICE. But that's from the danger bottle.
MOTHER. Just for tonight. We think you need to sleep.
ALICE. I do. Thank you, I ——
MOTHER. Here's your nightgown. Get ready for bed.
ALICE. At nine-thirty?
FATHER. Go on, go to bed early for once.
(Exit ALICE to bathroom. She puts on a different blouse for Scene Two, dons a floor-length nightgown for end of present scene.)
MOTHER. I'll just turn down her bed.
FATHER. Honey, I set it up with the insulator.
MOTHER. Really?
FATHER. I told them they could do it over the weekend. I'm sorry I didn't check with you first.
MOTHER. I wish you had, Doug.
FATHER. Helen, I had to decide quickly. Because of a cancellation, the insulator suddenly had this weekend free. You know how much more cheaply the house can be insulated during the summer. They'll work Saturday and Sunday straight through.
MOTHER. And what are *we* supposed to do?
FATHER. Go to my parents. We have a standing invitation. Dad's not feeling well. I'd like to see him. I think the children should see their grandparents, too.
MOTHER. It sounds like a good idea.
FATHER. You're not too put out that I didn't talk it over with you first?
MOTHER. Considering — I guess not. But Alice is supposed to go to a party this weekend.
FATHER. I'll talk to her tomorrow.

Act I   GO ASK ALICE   Page 23

MOTHER (crossing). I'll get Tim and Alexandria ready for bed. (Pauses at door.) Promise me you won't give another sleeping pill to Alice.
FATHER. I promise.
MOTHER. Unless, of course, the doctor prescribes them. Which isn't very likely at her age.

(Exit MOTHER. FATHER sits on Alice's bed, opens strongbox, removes diary, muses. Enter ALICE.)

ALICE. That's my diary, Dad.
FATHER. I wasn't going to read it.
ALICE. I'm not accusing you, Daddy.
FATHER. You're such a serious girl, putting your thoughts down on paper.
ALICE. I try to have *fun,* too.
FATHER. I wasn't being critical. Did you take the pill?
ALICE. Yes. Why do you keep the danger bottles in *my* bathroom?
FATHER. To make it less likely that Alexandria accidentally takes any of those pills. (FATHER exits to bathroom and puts bottle of pills back.)

(FATHER reenters.)

FATHER. Hop in bed and settle down. You'll start feeling drowsy in a few minutes. And no putting on the headphones tonight.
ALICE. I won't. Good night, Daddy. (She impulsively reaches up, kisses his cheek.)
FATHER. Good night, Alice. You're doing real well, keep it up. (FATHER exits. ALICE

finds her small flashlight, sits up in bed, her back to the door, and surreptitiously reads aloud from her diary.)

ALICE. "I guess I just can't be secure no matter what happens. I sometimes wish I were going with someone; then I'd always know I had a date and I'd have someone I could really talk to, but confidentially, no one has ever been that interested in me. I wish I were popular and beautiful and wealthy and talented." (She writes.) Am I some kind of a throwback? A misfit? A mistake! (ALICE puts her diary, flashlight away, settles down in bed, lies on her back, one arm stretched out beyond the bed.)

BLACKOUT

Act I   GO ASK ALICE   Page 25

Scene Two

LIGHTS: MOTHER and ALICE are talking in Alice's room. During blackout, ALICE pulled off nightgown, costume for this scene underneath.)

MOTHER. I hope we're doing the right thing.
ALICE. Mother, I'll meet the insulator in the morning when they come, give him the house keys. Take the bus and meet you at Grandfather's house. I wish you wouldn't make such a big deal out of it.
MOTHER. Does that party tonight mean that much to you?
ALICE. No, it doesn't mean *that* much to me. I just want to have some fun. My life is boring, boring, boring. (Horn honks.)
MOTHER. They're waiting. All right. Make sure you get on the right bus.
ALICE. There's only *one*.
MOTHER. Don't stay out too late. You didn't eat today. *Eat!*
ALICE. I will, Mom. 'Bye.
MOTHER. Good-bye, Alice. (MOTHER exits. ALICE picks up pen, speaks to it.)
ALICE. I think I'll write with you, Mr. Magoo, because you're the one who has the fun. (Writing.) Thank God today isn't another sock-in-the-belly day. I'm going to have fun! (ALICE has a mood change.) Oh, dear God, help me be accepted, help me belong, don't let

me be a social outcast. (Nervous, ALICE
puts diary away, jumps up and does a couple
of twirls. Front bell rings. She rushes to
door, opens it, speaks offstage.) Hi! Hi!
Come on in! (Offstage murmurs and "Hi's".)

(JILL enters.)

JILL. We waited until your parents' car turned the corner down the street. Are you sure it's okay?

(Enter ALICE, CHRIS, JOE, BILL and JAN.)

ALICE. It's okay, Jill.

(GLORIA speaks from doorway.)

GLORIA. Kitchen that way? (ALICE nods. GLORIA exits to kitchen.)

JOE. Jill's parents finked. They decided it was too hot for the symphony and stayed home.
BILL. Can't have any fun with the old folks hanging around.
JOE (starting routine). What's the younger generation coming to, hey?
BILL. Coming to? I think it just went. Down the drain.
JOE. Does it rain in your drain?
BILL. Yeah, it does. And it gives me a pain, to see it rain in my drain, which backs water up

in my main. (Obligatory laughter from the
others. ALICE joins in.)
JAN. Funny, funny guys, hey, Alice?
ALICE. Yes.
JAN. I'm Jan Fujara and this is Joe.
JOE. Joe Life-O Driggs.
ALICE (cheerily). Life-O?
JOE. Life-O-the-party. Group: laugh! (Everyone
laughs on cue. ALICE hesitantly joins in. JAN
exits for kitchen.)
BILL. I'm Bill Thompson and this is Chris
Vetrano.
ALICE. Hi, Chris.
CHRIS. Hi.
JILL. Is that your stereo?
ALICE. Yes, it's new.

(Enter GLORIA.)

JOE. Looks neat.
ALICE. Sit wherever you like. There's lots of
cushions.
BILL. I'll take this. (Sits in bean-bag chair. JILL
sits on floor, cross-legged, cool.)
GLORIA. Here, thirsty boy. (Hands JOE a Coke.)
JOE. Thanks, Gloria. (Whispers.) Fixed?
(GLORIA nods. JOE drinks, smiles at
ALICE, hands her Coke.) Drink? Or are
you afraid of my trench mouth?
ALICE. Of course not, Joe. Trench mouth sounds
fun.
GLORIA. We'll have the rest of the Cokes in a
few minutes. (Exit GLORIA.)
JILL. You heard any good jokes, Joe?
JOE. Yeah, I've got a new one. There was the

momma polar bear on one iceberg and the
baby polar bear on another one. And the two
icebergs kept moving further and further apart.
You know what the momma polar bear said?

JILL. No, what?

JOE. Radio! Radio! (Everyone laughs loudly except
CHRIS and ALICE.)

BILL. That was really funny! Almost tore my
head off!

JOE. What's wrong, Alice? Don't you like the
joke?

ALICE. I'm sorry, I didn't get it.

JOE. Didn't get it? Hey! Radio! Radio!
(More hilarity.)

ALICE. I don't get it. I'm sorry, I guess I'm stupid.

CHRIS (whispering). Alice, there's no joke.

JILL. Alice must be too sophisticated for our low
humor.

ALICE. I'm not sophisticated, honest.

JOE. Then go ahead and laugh. It's okay.

ALICE (chuckling). Well, if you say so . . .

CHRIS (whispering). They're testing you, Alice.

ALICE. What?

CHRIS. If you laugh you're a jerk.

JILL. What're you saying to her, Chris?

JOE. Maybe she's explaining the joke.

JILL. I think we're too low class for *both* of
them.

ALICE. No, honest.

JOE. No? No? You'd contradict a guest?

CHRIS. Lay off, Joe.

BILL. Hey, the radio joke is terrific, Joe. But I
like the feathers joke better.

JILL. The feathers joke! The feathers joke! Yeah,
tell that one.

Act I GO ASK ALICE Page 29

CHRIS. We don't wanna hear it.
JILL. "We?" You mean Alice can't speak for herself?
ALICE. I'd love to hear the feathers joke.
CHRIS. How's it going with the animated cartoons, Joe?
JOE. Don't get smart, Chris.
CHRIS. I'm not getting smart.
JOE. We're just starting out. We're not ready to take over Hollywood yet.
JILL. What about the feathers joke?
CHRIS. What are you working on *now?*
JOE. It's a Bugs Bunny cartoon. "Bugs Bunny Takes An Acid Trip." After that we're gonna do "Snow White The Drag Queen."
BILL (false laughter). I like it, I like it! What's your opinion, Alice?
ALICE. Sounds terrific!
CHRIS (whispering). Don't come on too strong with them.
JILL (looking through albums). How about some music?
ALICE. Sure. Anything you like.
JILL. If I could find something I like.
BILL. Fussy, fussy. How about this one?
JILL. Play it, Bill.
BILL. You command, I obey. (BILL and JILL dance, fairly slowly. They look well together, know it.)

(JAN sticks head in door.)

JAN. Where are the other two boys?
JILL. I don't know. They *said* they were coming.
JAN. If those guys no-show, I'm gonna be mad.

JOE. M-a-d!
JAN. Damn right!
JOE. Get mad! I'll handle you, Jan!
JAN (laughing). That's what I'm worried about! My handles! (Disappears.)
BILL. Wanna dance, Alice?
JILL. Go ahead.
ALICE. All right, Bill. (ALICE doesn't dance nearly so well with BILL as JILL, is very self-conscious. CHRIS quickly comes to her rescue.)
CHRIS. Dance with me, Prince Charming.
BILL. If you shake it.
CHRIS. Shake your own.

(After several moments, JAN and GLORIA enter, pass out Cokes.)

JAN. Cokes, everybody!
JOE. Gloria, give Alice and me fresh ones. We — (Meaningfully.) — polished off the other one.
JILL (turning stereo down). Tonight we're playing "Button, Button, Who's Got the Button?" You know, the game we used to play when we were kids.
BILL (stretching out next to ALICE). Only it's just too bad that now somebody has to baby-sit.
ALICE (puzzled). Baby-sit? (Takes sip of Coke.)
BILL. Sure. I might have to baby-sit you. But then you might have to baby-sit *me*.
ALICE. I'm confused.
BILL. It's dangerous not to have someone look after you.
JOE (purposely interrupting). Anyone's parents listen to Fifties records? Mine do. There's

Act I   GO ASK ALICE   Page 31

    always this guy with a deep voice who goes boo-wah. Boo-wah. Then he says, "Honey, I need you, I got to have you, if I don't have you I'll die of heartache." Alice, if I died right here, would you give me heart massage? (Everyone is sipping his Coke, staring intently at the others. ALICE senses that it has to do with the Cokes, sniffs hers.)

ALICE. Someone spike the Cokes?

BILL. No booze in mine.

JOE (insistently). Alice, I asked you a question. Would you give me a heart massage?

ALICE. Sorry. Well, I'd certainly try to, Joe.

JOE. How about *mouth-to-mouth* resuscitation?

ALICE (laughing nervously). Well, I suppose so.

JOE. Alice, you shouldn't laugh. It's not funny. You never know when someone is gonna keel over. People don't help each other enough in the modern world. They don't wanna get involved. I wanted to know if I dropped dead if you'd get involved.

ALICE (seriously). I'd get involved.

JOE. Thanks.

CHRIS. Leave her alone.

JOE. Hey!

ALICE. That's okay, Chris.

CHRIS. Are you all right?

ALICE. I feel funny.

CHRIS. Yours had acid in it.

ALICE. Had what?

BILL (pleasantly). Okay, Chris, butt out.

CHRIS. Be careful with her.

BILL. Relax, Chrissy.

ALICE. Bill? What's going on? I feel so strange.

BILL. Lucky you.

ALICE. Wha —— ?
BILL. Don't worry, I'll baby-sit you. This'll be
    a good trip. Come on, relax, enjoy it, enjoy
    it. (Carresses her face and neck.) Honestly,
    I won't let anything bad happen to you.
    Believe me, nothing bad, all good. (JOE is
    also affected. JAN administers to JOE.
    After several more moments of stillness,
    ALICE begins to laugh hysterically, her head
    in Bill's lap. JILL puts a rock record with
    a heavy beat on phonograph.)
ALICE. Snow White took Bugs Bunny's carrots!
    (ALICE jumps to her feet and begins to dance
    to the music. She dances much more
    confidently than before.) Radio! Radio!
    Feathers!
BILL (clapping). Yeah. Do it! Do it!
JOE (foggily). Alice for president!
JILL (laughing). Go ahead, Joe, dance!
JOE. I can't! The waves are all over me. They're
    taking me out — to sea!
ALICE. Dance with me, Bill!
BILL. I'd rather watch.
ALICE. I feel wonderful! Wonderful!
    Everything's happening at once! (The telephone
    rings. ALICE is unaware. JILL exits to
    answer it.)
GLORIA. I don't think we fixed those Cokes right.
    No one's getting anything out of them.
JAN. Didn't fix them right? Look at Alice and Joe.
    You just drank yours. Give it time. Alice
    and Joe drank their Cokes more than a half
    hour ago.
ALICE (laughing). What about the Cokes?
BILL. There's acid in some of the Cokes, we don't

Act I   GO ASK ALICE   Page 33

    know which. Except Gloria cheated and
    slipped one to you and Joe early.
ALICE. *Acid?* Then I —— . You mean I —— ?
    Wow! (Imitates man's voice.) Baby, I need
    you so much, boo-wah! If I don't have you,
    all the water in the clouds'll fall from my eyes!
    Hey! Hey! Baby, if you ever say good-bye,
    I will die. Boo-wah!

                (JILL enters.)

JILL. It's those two fink boys. They're at another
    party. Let's go!
JAN. Come on, Joe!
JOE. Wander yonder!
JILL. Gloria?
GLORIA. Ready! Let's go!
JILL (pushing GLORIA). Then move!
JOE. See ya later, vibrator!
BILL. Alice?
ALICE. Coming! (CHRIS holds ALICE back as
    BILL, JOE, JAN, GLORIA exit.)
CHRIS. In a minute.
JILL. Well?
CHRIS. We'll be over later.
JILL. You don't even know where it is.
ALICE. We're coming.
CHRIS. Where is it? At Phil's?
JILL. Yes. Five minutes from here.
CHRIS. We'll be right there.
JILL. Okay. See you later. Adieu, Alice.
ALICE (giggling). See you later. (JILL exits.
    Murmur of voices offstage. Front door slams.)
CHRIS. Sit down, Alice.
ALICE. Let's go to the party.

CHRIS. Maybe in a little while. After you come down.
ALICE. I don't *want* to come down. This is won-der-ful.
CHRIS. I know. I like to trip, too.
ALICE. I don't wanna miss the party.
CHRIS. Why don't *we* have one soon? But just for us girls? What do you think of that?
ALICE. It sounds great. Where?
CHRIS. My place is kinda tough on account of my parents.
ALICE. What about here? My parents won't object to a girls-only party.
CHRIS. We can't have any drugs with your parents around. But maybe *you* object to drugs, too?
ALICE. *Me?* (Laughs.) We'll wait until they're going out for a late night. My dad is always going to meetings and things.
CHRIS. Okay, sounds good.
ALICE. Do you know much about drugs?
CHRIS. Enough. What's on your mind?
ALICE. Nothing. Just thought I'd ask.

BLACKOUT

Act I GO ASK ALICE Page 35

Scene Three

LIGHTS: MOTHER and ALICE are in a discussion
   in Alice's room. In blackout, ALICE slipped
   on simple vest or neck scarf for costume change.
   CHRIS is in offstage kitchen, where she makes
   quick costume change.)

MOTHER. You're so "in" now, Alice. Everything
   about you is so *positive.* It's kind of exciting,
   even for me.
ALICE. I just managed to make a few friends, Mom.
MOTHER. A *few?* The phone hardly stops ringing.
ALICE. When you start out with no friends, a few
   seems like a lot.
MOTHER. And Jill Peters! Hers is one of the most
   respected families in this town. Father a town
   councilman, mother president of everything,
   her eldest son ——
ALICE (sarcastically). I know, Mom, they're
   examples for all of us.
MOTHER. Now don't get *negative.*
ALICE (laughing). Never.
MOTHER. And Jill coming to your party tonight.
   Well, your father's waiting. Don't forget to
   look in on Tim and Alexandria once or twice.
ALICE. I won't. We'll keep the stereo low.
MOTHER. Fine, fine.
ALICE. Adieu, Mom.
MOTHER. See you later tonight. Have fun. Tell
   Chris I'm sorry there wasn't more time to chat.

(MOTHER exits, CHRIS enters a moment later with hot coffee.)

CHRIS. Any problems?
ALICE. No. Mother was just gushing a little. At least it's better than hearing how my attitude determines my altitude.
CHRIS. Huh? (ALICE wordlessly takes vial from Chris's handbag.)
ALICE. Mind?
CHRIS. Why should I mind? We went in on it fifty-fifty. (CHRIS takes offered pill, both down them with coffee.) They take effect faster with hot coffee.
ALICE. I hate coffee.
CHRIS. Me, too.
ALICE. The girls are a little overdue.
CHRIS. Like three months.
ALICE. Was it *that* long ago we decided to have our girls-only party?
CHRIS. Right. Middle of July. Here it is the middle of October.
ALICE. Things came up. Like go-go-go thirty hours a day. Having practically all the boys at school chasing us!
CHRIS. Right! How *are* you, anyway?
ALICE. Wonderful! It's really been terrific since you got me a job in your boutique.
CHRIS. They like you. You work hard.
ALICE. I do? There's sure a lot of standing around.
CHRIS. You should see what some of the help does.
ALICE. You've really been good to me, Chris.
CHRIS. I don't know about that.
ALICE. If it hadn't been for you, I would never have met Richie. What a guy.

Act I GO ASK ALICE Page 37

CHRIS. I'm glad you two hit it off.
ALICE. Hit it off! The second time I was with him, he turned me on to speed! What a wonderful, crazy feeling. Wham! (Laughs.) I do everything backwards. I started on acid, then speed, then downers and tranks, *then* you showed me about uppers.
CHRIS. None too soon. You were bent out of shape.
ALICE. Was I! All those sleeping pills and tranquilizers were killing me.
CHRIS. Steal them from the medicine cabinet?
ALICE. Oh, no! I wouldn't do that! What am I saying? I *did* steal all my grandfather's sleeping pills. But I wouldn't take my dad's, I don't think. Anyway, when grandfather's ran out I gave the family doctor a long story and he finally prescribed some. But I was feeling *worse*. Then you gave me that upper the first day I was in your boutique. What a change!
CHRIS. You sure are the backwards kid. Most kids have pot first.
ALICE. Pot! Last week with Richie and his friend was the first time I ever smoked pot. (Laughs.) But like a complete idiot, I couldn't inhale the smoke and they had to get out a hookah pipe. Am I an amateur!
CHRIS. I don't know about *that*.
ALICE. How long have you been taking drugs?
CHRIS. More than a year.
ALICE. Every day?
CHRIS. Just about . . . I guess so . . . yes.
ALICE. I haven't missed a day since the party with the acid Coke. Learning

control is the thing. To get real high when you
want, and bring it down when you want.
CHRIS. Control gets harder. I wonder sometimes.
I always told myself I could get off drugs any
time I want. I never tried to get off. I'm
wondering if there might be a reason I haven't
tried.
ALICE. Because you like them. Why stop doing
something you like? If it feels good, do it.
CHRIS. Right. If it feels good, do it.

(Doorbell rings, ALICE flies to front door. JILL
enters followed by JAN and GLORIA.)

JILL. Sorry if we're late.
ALICE. You're not really late.
GLORIA. Your parents gone?
ALICE. Yes. And my brother and sister are in bed.
JAN. Good.
ALICE. I'll get the drinks.
GLORIA. We'll help. (Exit GLORIA, JAN, ALICE.)
JILL (accepting pill from CHRIS). I hear Alice is
a regular little doper.
CHRIS. That's not very friendly.
JILL. Is she?
CHRIS. Ask *her.* I'm her friend, remember?
JILL. You've been high so long you don't know
what it means to come down.
CHRIS. You're getting nasty, Jill. I don't like it.
JILL. Tut, tut. Chrissy is mad.
CHRIS. Why did you take up with Alice?
JILL. You mean there's something *wrong* with
her?
CHRIS. There's *nothing* wrong with her.
JILL. She has her uses.

CHRIS. What's that supposed to mean?
JILL. Let it mean whatever you *want* it to mean.
And get *off* my back. For a run-of-the-mill doper you can get presumptuous.
CHRIS. You do *use* people, Jill.
JILL. Look who's talking. Who's Alice's dope tutor? Where would Alice be without her older and wiser friend Chris to tell her when to take what?
CHRIS. I don't encourage her.
JILL. Of course not. You just stand around with the bag.

(ALICE enters, followed by JAN and GLORIA.)

ALICE. Hi! How come there's no music on?
JILL. Come on, slackers, put something on that phono. (Goes through albums.)
ALICE. Oh, Jill, my dad said to let you know you shouldn't have any problems getting into the university.
JILL. Honest?
ALICE. Honest. He's not in admissions and can't promise you, but he spoke to a certain person, and you're *in!*
JILL. Thanks for the good news. (Smirks at CHRIS.) It'll be a relief getting out of that high school and away from all those weird teachers. (JAN and GLORIA get pill from ALICE, who takes another for herself.)
GLORIA. They're not all weird.
JILL. They're all weird.
GLORIA. They have *some* really good teachers.
JILL. They're all bad teachers.
GLORIA. Okay, okay. I'm only telling the truth. But lies are okay. Whatever turns you on.

JAN. Mrs. Snarl is weird.
ALICE. Who?
JAN. You don't know Mrs. Snarl? That's right, you just transferred in this fall. She's the social adjustment counselor. Her name is Czarnl, C-z-a-r-n-l. We call her Snarl. You know what she said to me one day? "All teen-agers are bad. You are a teen-ager. Therefore, you are bad."
GLORIA. She didn't.
JAN. Honest to God, she did.
GLORIA. Could be. One day in the hall I heard her say to a greaser, "Corporal punishment may be against the law, but it's not against my inclinations."
CHRIS. How about: "Did you come here to go to school or to destroy the building in which your government gives you a place to learn?"
(All giggle and laugh.)
JAN. Hey, chocolate-covered peanuts!
ALICE. They're my very favorites. Take all you want.
JAN. Just a few. I have to watch my figure.
GLORIA. Why? Your boyfriend watches it.
JAN. That's not *all* he does. (General laughter, except cool JILL.)
JILL. What about Hose-nose? "Times are changing, young ladies. The military is not unfeminine. Consider the R.O.T.C."
GLORIA. Remember when Hose-nose marched into his own color guard during a parade?
(Laughter. JAN goes to bathroom with her purse.)
CHRIS. What about Mr. Chartreuse?
ALICE. Who's *that?*

Act I   GO ASK ALICE   Page 41

CHRIS. Mr. Chartres.
ALICE. The one who teaches biology?
CHRIS. Right. (Deep voice.) "Reproduction. Yes. It's a function universal among mammals. That's nothing to giggle about, young lady. All mammals reproduce, even I ... that is, ah ... yes ... well." (Much laughter.) Let's do a play.
JILL. Like what?
CHRIS. Let Gloria decide. She's an actress.
GLORIA. I was a sheep in a church play ––
JILL. Baa, baa.
GLORIA. Let me finish my credits. I was Robin Hood in ––
CHRIS. Let's do Robin Hood.
GLORIA. I don't remember.
CHRIS. Alice, you be Robin Hood.
ALICE. How about a knight errant?
GLORIA. A who?
CHRIS. Whatever. Go ahead.
ALICE. Pray, sire, let down the drawbridge so I might cross the moat, for I need succor.
GLORIA. What kind of sucker? All day or just the regular kind? (Girls giggle.)
JILL. I'll be the drama teacher: "Stay in character, Gloria."
GLORIA. Yes, Miss Strict.
JILL. Go on, continue the scene, please.
ALICE. I seek solace in a place without knavery.
GLORIA. No knaves here, sire. Only a nerd or two. (Giggles.)
JILL. You're breaking character again, Gloria.
ALICE. Prithee, what might a nerd be?
GLORIA. A nerd is an idiot or other person absurd.
ALICE. I pray there is no superabundance of nerds.

GLORIA. Only I and the king, sire. But let us speak of other matters.
ALICE. Good. Where is the fair princess?
CHRIS. Here I am, y'all!
JILL. You're out of character, Chris.
CHRIS. I'm sorry, Miss Strict. I'm a hilllbilly princess.
JILL. Not in *my* play, Miss Vetrano.
ALICE. Princess, I am weary from much traveling.
CHRIS. Oh, great knight, why dost thee travel?
ALICE. To find you, most fair.
CHRIS. Well, you found me, but you can't have me unless you slew a dragon.
ALICE. I just slew a few in the fog, fairest.
CHRIS. Have you proof?
ALICE. Here cometh the game-keeper.
GLORIA. Prithee, where is the slob who slew my dragons?
ALICE. I cannot tell a lie. I slew three with my little hatchet.
GLORIA. Oh, you did, huh? Well, I'm gonna slew you! (A pillow fight breaks out, with much giggling.)
JILL. High, higher, highest!
CHRIS (on all fours). High!
GLORIA (standing on Chris's back). Higher!
JILL (jumping on bed). Highest!
GLORIA (running). Fast!
CHRIS (following). Faster!

(JAN opens bathroom door.)

JAN. Fastest! Alice, come in, the mailman has a letter for you!
ALICE. What?

Act I GO ASK ALICE Page 43

JAN. Come on in!
JILL. Speed!
GLORIA. Speedier!
JAN. Speediest! (ALICE runs into bathroom,
 CHRIS stares after her.)
CHRIS (soberly). Let's put on some music.
JILL. Suit yourself.
CHRIS. How's this? Okay?
JILL. Whatever turns you on, Chris.
GLORIA. Hey, did you hear something outside?
JILL. With all the noise in here? (Pulls aside
 window curtain.)
GLORIA. I heard something.
JILL. There's no one out there, take it easy.
GLORIA. I think there is.
JILL. In this neighborhood?
GLORIA. Why not this neighborhood?
JILL. It's all Establishmentarian around here.
GLORIA. So what? The weirdos are coming out
 of the ground.
JILL. If you're so worried, go outside and take a
 look.
CHRIS. Come on, let's listen to the music.
JILL. Where's the speediest pair?
CHRIS. Still in the bathroom. Jan better have good
 stuff.
JILL. My, aren't we concerned.
CHRIS. Alice is my friend.
JILL. We all know that.

(ALICE and JILL run out of the bathroom, flushed.
 ALICE dabs trickle of blood on her arm with
 a bit of cotton as JAN aims her cotton at
 wastebasket.)

JAN. Music! Music!
CHRIS. It's on.
ALICE. Louder!
CHRIS. Okay!
ALICE. Come on! (JAN and ALICE start dancing. Others clap.)
JAN. Hey! Hey!
ALICE. Yeah! Yeah!
JAN. Hey! (The dancing becomes more frantic. ALICE loses her balance, sprawls on JILL.)
JILL. Damn you! (GLORIA turns down music.)
ALICE (giggling). I'm sorry!
JILL. You broke my nose!
ALICE (giggling). I didn't.
JILL. You clumsy idiot!
ALICE. I'm sorry.
JAN (laughing). She didn't mean it!
JILL. Look, Alice, if you can't handle the stuff, don't use it!
ALICE. Listen to Miss Prim.
JILL. I better get into that university. If I don't, someone's father is gonna get a phone call about his innocent daughter.
ALICE. It's nice to see you mad!
JILL (stalking out). You're damn right I'm mad.
ALICE. I'll see you to the door.
JILL. Don't bother. You better hope my nose isn't broken.
ALICE (laughing). I hope it isn't. (While ALICE exits with JILL, knocking starts on window in Alice's room.)
GLORIA. I knew someone was outside! (Screams.)
JAN. Wheee! Let 'em in!
CHRIS. Shut up!
ALICE (offstage). What's going on?

Act I   GO ASK ALICE   Page 45

GLORIA. Someone's out there! (JAN opens window.)

(JOE is at window.)

JOE. Thanks, baby! Hi!
GLORIA. This is a girls-only party.
JOE. We're integrating it! Come on, Bill!

(ALICE runs in.)

ALICE. Go to the front door. My parents are out.
JOE. Right! (ALICE runs to front door, CHRIS yells after her.)
CHRIS. Do you think you should?
ALICE (offstage). Why not?
JAN. Don't be a party-pooper, Chris.
CHRIS. Joe isn't always the nicest person to have around.
JAN. Don't be critical. Not everyone understands Joe.
CHRIS. *I* sure do.
GLORIA. All I can say is, he didn't have to scare us. I don't know why he couldn't go to the front door, even if he thought her parents *were* here.
JOE (offstage). Jan!
JAN. Joe! I love you! Come to me!
JOE. I'm coming!

(JOE runs into room.)

CHRIS. Not so loud! There's kids asleep upstairs.
JOE. Let 'em sleep. Hey, I missed you!

JAN. I missed *you*.
CHRIS. I didn't miss either of you.
JAN. It's all right *if* you shut up, Chris.

(Enter BILL.)

BILL. How's the party? Glad we're invited. Who's holding?

(ALICE enters.)

BILL. You holding, Alice?
ALICE (pointing at vial). Sure, take all you want.
BILL (picking it up). That's all you have?
ALICE. That's all.
JOE. I think you're speeding. Where'd you get it?
JAN. From me.
JOE. None for me?
JAN. We weren't expecting you, baby.
BILL. Anything else around?
ALICE. No, nothing else.
BILL. Richie didn't sell you anything else?
JOE. You didn't tell Bill you were seeing Richie.
BILL. It makes me mad, Alice.
ALICE. Look, we didn't agree to see just each other.
BILL (grabbing ALICE). I say we *did* agree.

(TIM enters.)

TIM. Leave her alone!
JOE. Yeah? Who the hell are you? (Grabs TIM, who grabs JOE low around the legs, pulls him off balance to the floor.) Hey!
BILL. Joe, you gonna let that kid whip your tail?
ALICE. Stop it!

Act I   GO ASK ALICE   Page 47

(ALEXANDRIA runs into the room.)

ALEXANDRIA. Leave my brother alone!
BILL (grabbing her from behind.) No, you don't!
    (JOE hits TIM in stomach. ALEXANDRIA
    bites Bill's hand.) Ouch!
JOE. Let's get out of here!
BILL. Come on! Move! (JAN races after JOE.
    BILL pulls GLORIA out.)
JOE. Thanks for the dope, Alice!
JAN. Sorry, Alice! These guys are crazy! See ya!
    (The four exit.)
ALICE. Timmy, Timmy, did they hurt you?
    (Comforts him.) Are you all right?
TIM. My stomach hurts.
ALICE. I'm sorry, I'm sorry. Are *you* all right,
    Alex?
ALEXANDRIA. I'm okay. Who were they?
CHRIS. They won't be back.
TIM. Did they hurt you, Alice?
ALICE. No, I'm fine.
TIM. Are you sure? Your eyes look funny.
ALEXANDRIA. They *do*. Are you sick?
ALICE. I guess I am, a little. Can you stand up,
    Tim?
TIM (getting up). How come that guy was gonna
    hurt you, Alice?
ALICE. He's crazy.
TIM. Oh.
ALICE. Don't worry. I'll never see him again.
    Come on, I'll put you two back in bed.
TIM. We can go ourselves. I think maybe someone
    should put *you* in bed.
ALICE. Maybe. Good night, then.
TIM. Good night. Come on, Alex.

ALEXANDRIA (kissing ALICE). Good night, Alice.
ALICE. Good night. Good night. Thank you. I love you. (ALEXANDRIA and TIM exit.)
CHRIS. I'm sorry, Alice.
ALICE. What for? It wasn't your fault.
CHRIS. You know what scares me?
ALICE. What?
CHRIS. What just happened seems normal.
ALICE. Huh?
CHRIS. When a doper wants his dope, you never know what's gonna happen.
ALICE. But that's only with the really hard stuff, isn't it?
CHRIS. Are you kidding? (ALICE has no answer, turns away.) I want to get off drugs.
ALICE. Really?
CHRIS. It's not just the drugs. It's the people you get mixed up with.
ALICE. But ——
CHRIS. I'm not talking about chippers, like Jill. I'm talking about people like Joe and Bill, Jan even.
ALICE. What you said about knowing you could stop, but never trying it, so how could you know? Look, if you want to stop, I want to stop with you just to know I can. I mean, I like drugs, I mean I *love* drugs, but where does that leave me if I have to have them and can't get them? You follow me? (CHRIS nods.) I'll stop with you.
CHRIS. I don't wanna try it here. It won't work. I have to go somewhere else.
ALICE. Are you sure?
CHRIS. I've got to get away from this scene. I'm going to the West Coast.

Act I GO ASK ALICE Page 49

ALICE. Maybe I'll go with you.
CHRIS. You can't do that.
ALICE. You're my friend. You're my only real friend. I used to have a friend, Beth. But she knows I'm using drugs and won't talk to me any more.
CHRIS. What's *her* thing?
ALICE. Books.
CHRIS. That's a new one.
ALICE. Books aren't so bad.
CHRIS. I didn't say they were.
ALICE. I want to go with you.
CHRIS. But I'm going tonight. (Pause.) Right now.
ALICE. I'm going with you, Chris. I can pack in a couple of minutes.
CHRIS. Are you *sure* you want to go? I mean, it's ——
ALICE. I'm sure.

BLACKOUT

END OF ACT ONE

ACT TWO

Scene One

LIGHTS: MOTHER is in Alice's room, opening a flat package. FATHER enters carrying a fat manila folder under his arm, which he drops on Alice's desk.)

FATHER. Oh, here you are.
MOTHER. What's that you're carrying?
FATHER. Some student exams. I thought I'd mark them in here. It's the quietest room in the house.
MOTHER. And nearest to Alice.
FATHER. What are *you* doing?
MOTHER. Fussing around, as usual. This is a plastic drop cloth painters use. I thought I'd try it out as a dust cover. Guess I'll put it over a chair. Or the bed?
FATHER. Dust cover? Aren't you being kind of pessimistic?
MOTHER. Optimism isn't working lately.
FATHER. But we finally got a letter from Alice last week. She sounded like she might be coming home.
MOTHER. Doug, it's been more than two months since she left with Chris. Christmas is only a couple of days away. If she were coming home, I'm sure she'd be here by now.
FATHER. Not necessarily. You know kids.
MOTHER. No, Doug. I *don't* know kids, it seems.
FATHER. Please don't cover that.

50

Act II   GO ASK ALICE   Page 51

MOTHER. I'm just trying to be practical.
FATHER. But there's something final about it. Like covering a body.
MOTHER. Douglas!
FATHER. I'm sorry! That was a crazy thing to say. I'm sorry! (MOTHER flees the room, FATHER runs after her. Offstage.) Helen, wait! Please!

(Lights go up on left portion of split set. FREDDIE and PEG are huddled near a space heater. FREDDIE is a teen-aged girl with short hair, leather jacket, heavy boots. PEG is thin, has stringy hair, is very nervous.)

FREDDIE. Man, I wish I had some grass, man. Anything, man.
PEG. I'll get paid in a couple of days, Freddie.
FREDDIE. I dunno if I can wait that long.
PEG. I'll have tips tonight.
FREDDIE. Tips? Who'd tip you?
PEG. I get tips, I get tips. I'm just sorry it comes from poor working-class people instead of the capitalists.
FREDDIE. Lemme see some of your tips.
PEG. I don't get much.
FREDDIE. I'm not fussy, man — quarters, dimes, nickels.
PEG. I don't have any right now. I have to eat, too, you know.
FREDDIE. Don't they feed you free in the restaurant?
PEG. There's only so much garbage I can eat.
FREDDIE. Yeah, man, yeah, man, you work in one smelly dump. I don't know what smells

worse, the food or the winos in there.

(Enter CHRIS.)

CHRIS. You're not so fragrant yourself.
FREDDIE. Hey! Don't get uptight.
CHRIS. Look, we've got work to do.
FREDDIE (pointing upstage through archway).
   Where'd you get the stereo in the showroom?
CHRIS. It's second-hand. We got it cheap from a *friend.*
FREDDIE. I'm not your friend?
CHRIS. Sure, Freddie.
FREDDIE. Thanks. I was *worried.* (Laughs, punches PEG, who obliges with echo laugh.)

(Enter ALICE.)

ALICE. Here's the velvet. Come on, you two, back away from the table, we've got work to do.
PEG. Sorry.
FREDDIE. You patching Santa Claus's pants? (Haw-haw laugh.)
CHRIS. First let's see how big these pieces are.
ALICE. One piece looks larger than the other.
FREDDIE. I hear Santa Claus won't come to San Francisco 'cause there's no snow for his sleigh.
PEG. Be quiet, Freddie.
FREDDIE. Go outside and yell at some capitalists.
ALICE. Why don't you two go in the showroom and watch TV.
FREDDIE. I don't like TV. I get flashbacks if the picture isn't adjusted right. (Haw-haw laugh.)
PEG (harsh whisper). That's enough, Freddie.

Act II GO ASK ALICE Page 53

FREDDIE. Quiet or I'll bat you.
PEG. I didn't mean anything.
CHRIS. Look, I've had about enough of you two.
FREDDIE. Okay, we'll cool it. How're you two capitalists doing?
CHRIS. We get by.
FREDDIE. Yeah? I don't see any customers.
CHRIS. They come in the evening mostly.
PEG (timidly). Where did you learn the boutique business?
ALICE. Back home. Chris and I worked in a boutique there.
CHRIS. And here in 'Frisco, too, till a few weeks ago.
FREDDIE. Soon's Peg gets paid, we'll buy some stuff from you.
CHRIS. Speaking of money, we told you the rules. If you hang out you have to pay fifty cents a Coke.
FREDDIE. We don't drink Coke.
ALICE. Then fifty cents for chair privileges. And you're not supposed to sit back here.
FREDDIE. I've got a chill. I need the heat, man. Back home all I ever heard about was San Francisco. Then I get here and it's so clammy I never get warm. Isn't that right, Peggy?
PEG. That's right. You never get warm. (Front doorbell of Asiatic cowbells, or the like, jingles. Exit CHRIS.)
FREDDIE. Hey, hey, hey. You got a big spender out there, man.
SHEILA (offstage). Chris! How nice to see you!
FREDDIE. Sounds like a free-loader.
CHRIS (offstage). Hello, Sheila.

(Enter SHEILA and CHRIS.)

SHEILA. Alice! How are you?
ALICE. Fine, Sheila, fine. (SHEILA is elegantly dressed in finery befitting a swinging woman in her thirties. She is tall, slender, wears dark glasses. She kisses Alice's cheek.)
SHEILA. You two disappeared! Chris, you didn't give me notice.
CHRIS. I know.
SHEILA. But of course you were in a rush to open your *own* boutique.
CHRIS. I'd rather not talk about it.
SHEILA. Alice, is Chris being rude? Maybe we should go out front where there's more privacy.
FREDDIE. Ignore us. We're dummies. Right, Peg?
PEG. Right, Freddie.
SHEILA. Your self-evaluation is accurate.
FREDDIE. Smart-mouthed broad.
SHEILA. Which *sex* are *you?*
FREDDIE. Watch it!
PEG. Sit down, Freddie. She's not worth it. She's corrupt.
SHEILA. Listen to the wretched little witch.
CHRIS. All right! Let's all relax. How'd you find us, Sheila?
SHEILA. One of our mutual friends was here in your shop a few days ago.
CHRIS. You mean Rod?
SHEILA. Yes.
CHRIS. Rod isn't a friend.
SHEILA. He looks upon *you* as a friend.
CHRIS. What do you want, Sheila?

Act II GO ASK ALICE Page 55

SHEILA. I'm not angry that you left without notice.
CHRIS. What's on your mind?
SHEILA. I'm giving a party tonight, and I just thought ——
ALICE. Forget it, Sheila.
SHEILA. But what's wrong?
ALICE. I don't know how you can even *ask*. I've still got bruises on me from your other "party."
SHEILA. Did you fall? Is that what happened?
CHRIS. Don't act dumb, Sheila. You know very well what happened. You and Rod gave smack to Alice and me.
FREDDIE. Wish I had some smack, man.
ALICE. I'm not sure what you and Rod did to us. I don't want to know!
SHEILA. I'm sure you're mistaken.
CHRIS. The hell we are, pervert.
SHEILA. This is absurd.
ALICE. Your parties! The first one we were at the smoke was so thick we got high just smelling it.
SHEILA. So?
ALICE. So Chris and I came out West to stay straight. We started using again the night of your party.
SHEILA (amused). Oh, really?
FREDDIE. Who wants to get straight, man?
ALICE. Shut *up!*
SHEILA. Who ever heard of a party without pot?
ALICE. We're not complaining about the pot.
SHEILA. You sound like it.
ALICE. It's what you and Rod did to us! You set us out on a low with smack, then you and Rod got high on speed. You planned it all! Sadists!

Perverts! (Crying.) Get out! Get out!
SHEILA. Good-bye! Pot-heads! (SHEILA exits. Doorbell jingles.)
PEG. When it comes, her kind'll be the first to go.
CHRIS. When what comes?
PEG. Thesis, antithesis, synthesis. Society, putrid with disease, is poised at this moment at antithesis. (Bolder:) You may not be aware of it, but society is disintegrating. The pillars of the body politic are about to crash down upon all our shoulders.
FREDDIE. Amen.
PEG. But something *can* be done! We can recognize the state of decay that all the Sheilas signify! Recognition is the necessary condition to action! Action! We must throw aside all outmoded values and destroy everything! Everything! Even if it's daughter against mother, son against father! Action! Revolution! Now! (PEG stands rigidly, her whole woebegone body shaking. FREDDIE leads her out.)
FREDDIE. Come on, Peg, let's hit the road. Come *on,* Peggy. (PEG is in a daze, FREDDIE has to prod her out. Jingle from doorbell.)
ALICE. Chris, I'm going bananas.
CHRIS. I know, I know! We come out here, get jobs. Put a little money together, open a store, and it's crazy.
ALICE. I feel awful!
CHRIS. Own your own business, the American dream.
ALICE. Chris, this isn't a business! There's no heat. The ceiling's coming down. And there's rats! God, are they big! (They

Act II   GO ASK ALICE   Page 57

cling to one another.)
CHRIS. I can't take much more.
ALICE. I can't either. What should we do? Go back?
CHRIS. I've been thinking about it . . .
ALICE. Yes?
CHRIS. Come on. Let's not be quitters. Let's refinish the stereo with the red velvet. Where's the gold thumbtacks?
ALICE. Out in the showroom. But ——
CHRIS. Let's not talk right now. Come on.
ALICE. Okay, but ——
CHRIS. Come on.

(CHRIS exits, followed by ALICE. Simultaneously, FATHER enters bedroom, followed by MOTHER.)

FATHER. You know I didn't mean that drop cloth thing the way it sounded. Don't you, honey?
MOTHER. Yes, Doug. I'm over-reacting to everything lately.
FATHER. Guess I'll start marking those exams.
MOTHER. Will it disturb you if I do some cleaning in here?
FATHER. No, not at all. The exams are just multiple choice. Monkey work.
MOTHER. Her room isn't very dirty. Maybe just a light going over with the dust mop.
FATHER. I wonder how clean it is where Alice is at.
MOTHER. I'm more worried about her diet. All the articles you read say how teen-agers who run away are always malnutritioned.

(FATHER picks up manila folder, then angrily slams it down on desk.)

FATHER. You know, I keep hearing that the family is disintegrating. I don't feel disintegrated... a little disorientated, yes, but disintegrated, no.

MOTHER. You're doing just fine, Doug.

FATHER. What's disintegrating? We have a home, an adequate income, we love our children, so what's the problem?

MOTHER. I don't know, Doug.

(MOTHER pats FATHER on shoulder, exits for dust mop. CHRIS enters for piece of velvet left on table, ALICE standing in archway.)

CHRIS. And don't forget parents. Parents were part of the reason I ran away. My parents would never listen to anyone but themselves.

ALICE. A lot of people still say children should be seen and not heard.

CHRIS. That's stupid.

ALICE. I know it is.

CHRIS. That's why so many problems start. Parents won't let their kids talk.

ALICE. You've got a point.

CHRIS. All my parents do is harp and preach. And nag! Always negative! Don't do this, don't do that! Yack, yack, yack.

ALICE. My parents treat me like a child but expect me to act like an adult. Yackity, yack, yack.

CHRIS. That's right! You hit the ol' nail on the bazoo.

ALICE. They give me orders like I'm a little

Act II GO ASK ALICE Page 59

    animal to be trained.
CHRIS. Or a robot!
ALICE. Right! Then they turn around and want the robot to think for itself.
CHRIS. I agree. If parents want kids to make mature judgments, they have to treat them like mature people.
ALICE. Parents want everything *their* way. But it doesn't work that way.
CHRIS. It sure doesn't. Parents are selfish, that's what.
ALICE. I'm gonna write some of this down, *now*.
CHRIS. A good idea. I'll just tack this on the stereo.

(Exit CHRIS. ALICE gets strongbox with diary from under chair, writes while she munches on dried cereal from box. Enter MOTHER with dust mop.)

MOTHER. Doug, I was just reading the other day —— Oh, sorry, am I interrupting you?
FATHER. No. Go ahead.
MOTHER. A psychiatrist or someone had an article in the paper. He said that today's children are different because they act out. Whereas previous generations of children didn't act out.
FATHER. No?
MOTHER. No. They got depressed.
FATHER. Depressed?
MOTHER. Yes. He says that's what's happening to yesterday's kids today. They made a lot of trouble for society in their teens, now in their twenties and thirties they get despondent

and can't function.
FATHER. Huh. I was reading somewhere, too, that our society worships teens. Adults dress like teen-agers, wear their hair the same way, listen to the same music, even try to assimilate the same values. Here kids are looking for adult models, and adults are aping kids!
MOTHER. That has the ring of truth.
FATHER. You know something? We're afraid of kids. We're afraid to say "no" to them.
MOTHER. Now, Doug ——
FATHER. No! I mean it! Kids have to be told to do certain things once in a while. Maybe we weren't firm enough with Alice.
MOTHER. Doug, please.

(MOTHER goes to FATHER and puts her arms around him. ALICE throws her diary down and stands, hollers through archway at CHRIS.)

ALICE. Chris, what we've been saying makes a lot of sense to me! You know what it all adds up to? Your parents, my parents, don't care about us!
FATHER. What in God's name does Alice have against us? What did I do to her? Doesn't she care about us?

(CHRIS enters.)

CHRIS. You're right, Alice. Parents don't care.
MOTHER. I'm sure Alice cares.
ALICE. All parents want are kids they can brag about!

Act II   GO ASK ALICE   Page 61

FATHER. She's run away. Is that caring?
CHRIS. Bragging about your kids isn't caring!
ALICE. It certainly isn't!
MOTHER. She's all mixed up, Doug.
ALICE. Chris?
CHRIS. What?
FATHER. I miss her, I miss her, I miss her. Oh, God.
ALICE. Chris, I miss home so much.
MOTHER. I miss her, too.
ALICE (tearfully). Chris, I can't stand it any more. I've got to call home.
MOTHER. Don't mark any more papers. Come on, let's go in the kitchen.

(CHRIS exits through archway, reenters with telephone on extension, hands it to ALICE.)

ALICE. I finally learned how to direct dial long distance.
FATHER. Maybe it wasn't a good idea to come in here.
MOTHER. Nothing seems like a good idea any more.
FATHER. I wish I knew what to *do!*
    (MOTHER and FATHER embrace. Telephone rings, MOTHER exits to answer it.)
ALICE. Mom! Mom!

(MOTHER reenters Alice's room with telephone on extension.)

MOTHER. Alice! Oh, Alice!
FATHER (grabbing telephone). Alice!
ALICE. Daddy! Daddy! I miss you!

FATHER. We miss *you!* (Inanely:) We got your letter!
MOTHER (taking telephone). Are you all right?
ALICE. I'm fine! Momma? Momma?
MOTHER. Yes?
ALICE. Can I come home?
MOTHER. Please come home!
FATHER (grabbing telephone). Come home! Please!
ALICE. Thank you! Thank you!
FATHER. I'm coming to get you! Where are you?
ALICE. San Francisco.
FATHER. I'll be right there!
ALICE. San Francisco, *California.*
FATHER. Here, your mother wants to talk to you.
    (FATHER gives MOTHER telephone, charges from room.)
ALICE. Mom, I'm sorry. I'm really, really sorry. Can you forgive me?
MOTHER. There's nothing to forgive. Have you been eating?
ALICE (reading label on cereal box). Sure. A lot of protein.
MOTHER. Good. I'm glad to hear *that.*

(FATHER reenters.)

FATHER. Just happen to have a couple of airline schedules. (He has a whole handful, of every airline.) Let's see, there's a direct flight to San Francisco in an hour and a half. An hour and a half! (Grabs telephone, schedules spill out of his hand.) Sit tight, Alice! I'm flying in an hour and a half!
ALICE. Honest? Honest?

Act II   GO ASK ALICE   Page 63

FATHER. Meet me at the airport. If there's any problem, we'll both call Mother here and she'll tell me where you're at. Good-bye.

ALICE. Good-bye, Daddy! Good-bye! Thank you! I love you! (Both hang up. ALICE sits stunned.)

FATHER. Drive me to the airport?

MOTHER. Of course.

FATHER. My credit cards are in my wallet. (MOTHER and FATHER exit. ALICE snaps out of it.)

ALICE. Chris! None of us mentioned you. How awful! You're flying back with us, of course.

CHRIS. Alice, I cheated. I got in touch with my parents last month. You know what? They've moved. To another part of the country. I'll call them later today.

ALICE. You *are* going back. Aren't you? You should go to them.

CHRIS. I guess so. Yeah. Try it again.

ALICE. Call them now.

CHRIS. Later, Alice. We've got to get you to the airport. The way traffic is, it'll probably take as long for the limousine or bus to get there as for your dad to fly here.

ALICE. There's time, Chris. Phone your parents now.

CHRIS. No, Alice. It's okay. I'll leave tomorrow, or the next day.

ALICE. You sure?

CHRIS. I'm sure. I'm not gonna stay *here* and wrestle a rat.

ALICE. Call *me* tomorrow. I'll wait by the phone all day.

CHRIS. I'll call.

ALICE. You promise?
CHRIS. I promise. (ALICE throws her arms around CHRIS, sobs.)
ALICE. Good-bye, Chris. I love you. You're the best friend I ever, ever had.
CHRIS (fighting tears). Come on. Let's find out how to get to the airport. Then we'll call your mother and find out what the hell flight your father is on. So we'll know where to find him.

(Exit CHRIS and ALICE. MOTHER reenters Alice's room, picks up dust mop, wastebasket. Suddenly she impulsively dumps wastebasket on the floor. She stares at her deed for several seconds, then stoops and picks up the crumpled papers, puts them back in wastebasket. She shouts through open door at offstage FATHER, as she picks up airline schedules.)

MOTHER. Don't forget your raincoat!
FATHER (offstage). All right!
MOTHER. Remember to call as soon as you meet Alice!
FATHER (offstage). I will!
MOTHER. Take the first flight back!

(FATHER appears in doorway.)

FATHER. All right! All right! You order me around like a kid!

BLACKOUT

Act II   GO ASK ALICE   Page 65

Scene Two

LIGHTS: MOTHER is in Alice's room.
ALEXANDRIA enters.)

ALEXANDRIA. Hi, Mom, whatcha doing?
MOTHER. I'm measuring the walls.
ALEXANDRIA. What for?
MOTHER. I'm thinking of wall papering . . . or
    maybe painting, I don't know which.
ALEXANDRIA. Oh. Where's Alice?
MOTHER. You keep coming into her room.
ALEXANDRIA. She didn't go away again, did she?
MOTHER. Alexandria! Alice came back from
    California *months* ago.
ALEXANDRIA. So? She didn't say anything when
    she left before.
MOTHER. Is that why you keep coming in here?

(Enter FATHER.)

FATHER. There you are, Alexandria. This is a
    wonderful report card. Wonderful!
ALEXANDRIA (shyly). I even got an A in math.
FATHER. Marvelous!
ALEXANDRIA. Don't tell Alice I got straight
    A's, okay? (ALEXANDRIA runs from room.)
FATHER. Kids.
MOTHER. Would you hold the end of this tape
    measure? Thanks.
FATHER. I'd like to talk to you, honey.
MOTHER. I wish this tape were longer than six feet.

FATHER. Helen? Could you stop for a minute?
MOTHER. Just let me put a pencil mark here. All right. What's on your mind?
FATHER. George. He's unreal.
MOTHER. He's a nice young man.
FATHER. He makes *me* look like a radical.
MOTHER. Would you rather she were dating Joe Driggs or that Richie person she was going out with last year? Or Bill Thompson?
FATHER. Misfits.
MOTHER. Well, there you are.
FATHER. But isn't there something in between? Aren't there any ordinary American boys left?
MOTHER. Give her time.
FATHER. How much time does she need?
MOTHER. She's getting back into things. The phone is ringing again. I don't think she'll be going out with George much more.
FATHER. Now wait. Let her go out with George. But can't there be a little *variety?* Like Joel Reems. Why can't she go out with him?
MOTHER. First time I've heard that name. Who's Joel Reems?
FATHER. A student at the university.
MOTHER. Alice dating college boys? (Front door slams.)
FATHER. The kid's barely eighteen.
ALICE (offstage). Hello, house!
MOTHER. In here! Do you suppose George is with her?
FATHER. I would imagine.

(Enter ALICE with GEORGE, the latter dressed very conservatively.)

Act II   GO ASK ALICE   Page 67

MOTHER. Back from the concert already?
ALICE. Mother, you know I have to baby-sit soon.
FATHER. Hello, George!
GEORGE. Good evening, Doctor Aberdeen!
ALICE. Mom, I found some of that material you were looking for.
MOTHER. Oh, where is it?
ALICE. I left it on the front hall table. Thanks again for the chocolate-covered peanuts, George. I can't fight temptation any longer. (She eats several pieces.)
GEORGE. But, Alice, I ——
MOTHER. Nice to see you again, George.
GEORGE. Thank you, ma'am. (MOTHER and ALICE exit.) Funny she's so sure I gave her the peanuts.
FATHER. They were delivered this noon, just before you came for her. Alice thought she recognized your handwriting on the card.
GEORGE. If she wants to insist they're from me, I'll accept the honor. Anyway, it's a privilege to take Alice places, Doctor Aberdeen.
FATHER. I wish you wouldn't call me doctor.
GEORGE. Excuse me, sir, I thought you took your doctorate.
FATHER. I did, but "doctor" sounds pretentious to me.
GEORGE. *I see.*
FATHER. Every time someone calls me doctor I think I should be taking a pulse.
GEORGE (laughing). That's rather humorous, sir.
FATHER. Yes.
GEORGE. Well.

FATHER. Well, George, do you have a career goal?
GEORGE. Of course, sir. It's never too early to plan ahead these days.
FATHER. I agree.
GEORGE. I'm going into the field of alternate energy, sir.
FATHER. Uh-*huh*.
GEORGE. Solar energy, to be exact. If you don't mind my saying so, sir, this house of yours is a prime, repeat, *prime* candidate for conversion to solar heat.
FATHER. Really?
GEORGE. Not total conversion, mind you. There's not enough annual sunlight in this region for that. But I think at least sixty per cent of your annual heating requirement could easily be furnished by the sun.
FATHER. That's great. (Telephone rings.)
ALICE (offstage). I'll get it!
GEORGE. By the time I'm twenty-one I plan on having my own company. I hope you'll be one of my first customers.
FATHER. I hope so, too. That's quite a goal you've set for yourself.
GEORGE. I don't know, sir. I've been planning since I was thirteen.
FATHER. Thirteen?

(Enter ALICE, returning phone to cradle in doorway.)

GEORGE. Well, Alice, I enjoyed the concert a great deal. The strings and woodwinds were, I thought, especially effective.
ALICE. Not to mention the percussion. (In background, FATHER almost laughs out loud,

Act II   GO ASK ALICE   Page 69

clamps hand over mouth.)
GEORGE. Yes. Beethoven's "Sixth" was never more zestfully done, I'm sure. Good evening, then.
ALICE. I'll take you to the door.

(MOTHER appears in doorway.)

MOTHER. Leaving, George?
GEORGE. Yes.
MOTHER. I'll see him out. (Exit GEORGE and MOTHER.)
FATHER. Alice, why do you go out with George?
ALICE. He's safe. He wouldn't know *what* to do if you passed him a joint.
FATHER. Please don't say joint.
ALICE. O-*kay*. All I meant was, George is out of the drug scene, where I want to *stay*. At least with him I don't have to worry.
FATHER. Is the temptation that great?
ALICE. You think I'm a dope fiend. Go ahead, admit it.
FATHER. Alice!
ALICE. I'm not an addict, Dad. I don't have any problems stopping when I want to. I don't go through withdrawal. It's just that it's so easy for me to start. Jesus, every time I get a whiff of smoke somewhere, things inside me start going around again . . .
FATHER. I didn't know it was so difficult for you.
ALICE. Believe me, Dad, I sure don't want to go back to living from one upper to the next.
FATHER. I wish you wouldn't use that drug terminology.
ALICE. Skip the terminology. I have a drug

problem. I know that. I'm working through it, getting back to being normal.

FATHER. You seem to be doing all right. Your mother says you're "in" again. The phone rings all the time.

ALICE. Dad, they're dopers. They think I'm holding, that I have drugs to sell them. Understand?

FATHER. But you obviously don't have any. Do you?

ALICE. I don't think you trust me. Not that I blame you, with me starting back on drugs again so soon after you brought me home from San Francisco.

FATHER. And stopping again, too. And on your *own.* (ALICE shrugs.) It's true we didn't trust you, watching you all the time. Sending Tim or Alexandria along with you to the store and so forth. But we've stopped all that.

ALICE. You took the sleeping pills out of my medicine cabinet.

FATHER. Well. All right. We did.

ALICE. I've never taken a single pill of any kind from this house.

FATHER. I believe you.

ALICE. And in case you've ever wondered, I've never touched a bottle in the house. I'm not even sure what alochol tastes like, except champagne.

FATHER. Keep it that way.

ALICE. Why did you hide the sleeping pills?

FATHER. I was concerned.

ALICE. All right. You've got a point. But *my* point is saying you trust me doesn't make

much sense when you hide pills.
FATHER. I'll put them back.
ALICE. I don't mean that. You can hide them if you want, just as long as we're honest with each other.
FATHER. I'll put them back. I trust you and I mean it.
ALICE. It's your decision. (FATHER puts his arm around her.) I love you. Do you love me, Daddy?
FATHER. Very, very much.
ALICE. All I do is cause you problems.
FATHER. That's what living is for: problems.
ALICE. Does Mother love me?
FATHER. Of course.
ALICE. Then why doesn't she stop her housework and tell me once in a while?
FATHER. Do you ever tell her you love her?
ALICE. It's hard to.
FATHER. Why, for heaven's sake?
ALICE. There's kind of a distance between us. I think I'm supposed to be someone else, cheerful, outgoing, meeting challenges. What a word, challenge. "That girl will do well, she likes a challenge."
FATHER. Who says that?
ALICE. Everyone. What about people who don't want a challenge? Isn't there any room for us? Are we rejects, discards? (Doorbell rings.)
FATHER. Your mother'll answer it.
ALICE. That's probably Joel.
FATHER. Joel Reems?
ALICE. Yes. I left one of my books behind at the library. He's returning it. He just phoned a few minutes ago.

Page 72   **GO ASK ALICE**   **Act II**

FATHER. Does he know you're in high school?
ALICE. He does now. I explained to him I'm allowed to use the university library because you're on the faculty. (Smiles.) He doesn't relate to me like a teeny-bopper.
FATHER (smiling back). Good. Hope you see more of each other.

(JOEL stands tentatively in doorway.)

FATHER. Come on in, Joel, we were just talking about you.
ALICE. And none of it good.
JOEL. That's a break. Now I've got nowhere to go but up.
FATHER. How's the job at school, Joel?
JOEL. Okay. Really okay. A real body builder, shoveling all that coal. I didn't think there were any coal-burning furnaces left.
FATHER. Maybe you'll give the college a solar heating system when you're rich.
JOEL. Number one on my list.
FATHER. Fine, fine.
ALICE. Thanks for bringing back my book, Joel.
JOEL. That's okay. Glad to do it. (FATHER crosses, winking at ALICE on way out, making sure he leaves her door wide open. JOEL feels awkward in situation.)
ALICE. How do you like my room?
JOEL. It's classic. You sure I should be in here?
ALICE. Relax. Dad knows you're here.
JOEL (giving her book). I'm supposed to give you the book and say good-bye to *him* at the front door. Right?
ALICE. Joel, my door's open.

Act II   GO ASK ALICE   Page 73

JOEL. Your dad's outside it with a shotgun, right?

ALICE. Dad likes you.

JOEL. He does? He doesn't know me very well. He probably thinks it's strange for a college freshman seeing a high school girl. Maybe you do, too. Look, I'm not exactly a dirty old man. I just turned eighteen. I'm what they call an accelerated student.

ALICE. I'll be seventeen soon. (Teasing.) To me you're just a child because I'm quite sophisticated, you know.

JOEL. How is jet-setting these days?

ALICE. I get frightfully tired of the same glamorous faces. It's boring, boring, boring. That's why I'm so enchanted with you, young fellow. You're so different from the others. You're ugly.

JOEL. Hey! (Both laugh.)

ALICE. Joel?

JOEL. Yeah.

ALICE. Thank you for letting me tell you things about myself.

JOEL. You took some drugs. You've had some problems. So?

ALICE. It's not necessarily that simple. The dopers are pressing me, Joel. They won't leave me alone. They call me Nancy Nice and Mary Pure because I quit. They come up to me in the halls at school and invite me to parties. I've been threatened. Some crazy boy grabbed me in the park.

JOEL. That's awful. What does your dad say?

ALICE. He doesn't know any details. And I don't want to give you any more details. You have your own problems.

JOEL. Don't worry about it. Tell me whatever you want.

ALICE. It gets scary. I baby-sit for this Mrs. Larsen person. That's where I'm going in a little while. Anyway, one night baby-sitting this Jan Fujara just walked right in the house and was she high, I mean, like stoned right out of her gourd. She wanted to baby-sit in my place to earn some money. I couldn't talk to her at all. Then I got afraid that her yelling might wake the baby, or that Jan might even *do* something. She wouldn't leave. I didn't want to call the police so I called her parents. They came and got her. They thanked me because Jan's on parole. But Jan hates me. She calls me Miss Fink Mouth and all kinds of things.

JOEL. I know you're trying to, but you don't scare me. I want to keep seeing you and phoning you. Do you think it might be all right if I phoned you every night?

ALICE. Will you do it if you say you're going to do it?

JOEL. Absolutely.

ALICE. Please call me every night.

JOEL. Right now I want to get out of here before your dad or mom come in. I'm not a prude or anything, but I don't ——

(Enter TIMOTHY.)

TIM. Hey, who are you?
ALICE. He's leaving.
TIM. Leaving?

Act II   GO ASK ALICE   Page 75

ALICE. 'Bye, Joel. Let yourself out, okay?
JOEL. Sure. (Exit JOEL.)
ALICE. What's on your mind, Tim?
TIM. Nothing. Who's Joel?
ALICE (ignoring question). Why did you come in here?
TIM. I don't know. Should I leave?
ALICE. I suppose you wanna listen to my stereo.
TIM. I like having you home. (Affected, ALICE turns away.)
ALICE. I've been back for a long time, Timmy.
TIM. Please don't go again.
ALICE. I won't. Ever.
TIM. I know you just had a nightmare about Gramps.
ALICE. How?
TIM. Jeez, there was a lot of commotion. Then you and Mom walked around in the yard in the middle of the night. I could hear you through my window.
ALICE. Oh.
TIM. I'm sorry. I didn't know Gramps that well, but *you* did.
ALICE. I grew up with Gran and Gramps. Before we moved here. It was like having extra parents.
TIM. Are you sleeping okay now?
ALICE. Yes.
TIM. Are you sure?
ALICE. Tim, do you ever think about ––? I mean, this is gonna sound weird to you, but I was thinking about embalming.
TIM. Me, too.
ALICE. You're being nice.
TIM. No. Honest to God, I wonder what they do.

ALICE. Do you? (TIM nods.) I was thinking of taking a book from the library.
TIM. Me, too.
ALICE. Tim, stop it.
TIM. No, seriously. You always hear about embalming but no one ever explains it to you.
ALICE. The body still eventually decays. My nightmare was about all the worms eating Grandfather's body.
TIM. I know, I heard.
ALICE. I don't understand resurrection. Of course, I don't understand electricity or television or anything else, for that matter. But how can God put a body together after it's all decayed and fallen apart?
TIM. Well . . .
ALICE. Wait a minute, I didn't finish. You know what I thought then? I thought of a how a brown, shriveled little gladiola bulb can blossom. So if *that* can happen, why can't there be resurrection?
TIM. That's a good point.
ALICE. You're not just humoring me?
TIM. Of course not. You're too smart to put anything over on.
ALICE. Smart? Me? Look who gets the grades.
TIM. I'm a grind, Alice. I'm getting sick of it. I look around school and see the kids goofing off, and I wonder what I'm doing.
ALICE. Let them goof off. You stay with your books.
TIM. It really gets to be a drag.
ALICE. You know I've had some problems with drugs.
TIM (embarrassed). Well, sure —— I mean, gee

Act II   GO ASK ALICE   Page 77

whiz, Alice.

ALICE. All right, all right. And thank you for never putting me down. But that wasn't what I wanted to say. Tim, take it from *me,* stay away from drugs.

TIM. Geez, Alice, I wasn't planning anything. I was just complaining about the study grind.

ALICE. Drugs are all around you, Tim. Kids want you to take them, they want to sell them to you, because that's how they make their money. Tim, I sold acid to grade school kids once. Promise me you won't start taking drugs.

TIM. Please, Alice. Don't get so worked up. I'm okay, I'm okay. I'm no more thinking about drugs than I am hijacking a jet.

ALICE. I'm sorry. I never thought I'd turn into an Establishmentarian. (Doorbell rings.)

TIM. I'll get it.

ALICE. That must be Marge to take me to Mrs. Larsen's. (While TIM is gone, ALICE gathers a few objects to take along.)

TIM (offstage). Alice! It's for you!

ALICE. Is it Marge?

(Enter JAN.)

JAN. No, me. Hi, Alice! Just thought I'd stop by. (ALICE stares at her.) Mind if I come in?

ALICE. Come in.

JAN. You're wondering why I'm here.

ALICE. Well?

JAN. I came to apologize, bury the hatchet, pass the peace pipe or whatever honest injuns do. Shake my hand? I know now you were just

trying to help me. Man, I was out of my head.
I could have hurt that baby, right? You could
have called the cops, right? But you didn't,
right? You called my parents. I was really,
but really, mad about that. I know now how
stupid I was. Us kids have been on your back,
Alice. We know that. We're getting off.

ALICE. It hasn't been so bad.

JAN. Sure it has. We know it, too.

ALICE. Well, okay.

JAN. Did you get my peace offering? The chocolate-covered peanuts?

ALICE. They're from you? How did you know I like them so much?

JAN. From that party a long time ago.

ALICE. You mean our girls-only party? You remember from that? (ALICE is touched.)

JAN. Sure. Honest injuns never forget. We've had a lot of good times together, Alice. Speaking of good times, have you heard from Chris?

ALICE. She's starting college this fall.

JAN. Great. Anyway, I'm sorry for the hard times, and thanks for the good times.

ALICE. Thank *you*. Why didn't you sign the card?

JAN. I was afraid you'd throw the candy in the garbage if you knew it was from me. (Honking outside.)

ALICE. Oh, oh. *That's* my ride to Mrs. Larsen's.

JAN. The Larsen's: where you had to call my parents. Isn't that irony or something?

ALICE. I guess so.

JAN. Hey! Don't act guilty. Go baby-sit. Don't keep your ride waiting. No hard feelings, really.

ALICE. Really?

JAN. Really. I mean it. So long, Alice. Glad you like the peanuts. Have any yet?

Act II GO ASK ALICE Page 79

ALICE. Yes. Before. Tell Marge I'll be right out, okay?
JAN. Okay! Enjoy your trip — I mean, your ride. (JAN exits.)

(More honking. ALICE unlocks her strongbox, takes out diary. More honking. In mid-stride, ALICE stops and shakes her head, sits on bed. Moments pass, enter MARGE.)

MARGE. I'm sorry to barge in but we're late.
ALICE (monotone). Didn't Jan tell you I was coming right out?
MARGE. Jan said something filthy to me.
ALICE. Oh? Just a sec, Marge. I'll be right with you.
MARGE. Hurry up, for God's sake. (ALICE puts her hands to her face.) Now what's the matter?
ALICE. Maybe you better get another baby-sitter.
MARGE. Aren't we fickle? Come on, Alice, let's go.
ALICE. Oh, God.
MARGE. What? What was that?
ALICE (pitching face down on bed). No . . .
MARGE. What's wrong?
ALICE. I can't baby-sit.
MARGE (angrily). Now just a minute.
ALICE (screaming). Honest injun!
MARGE (frightened). Okay, Alice. Then don't.
ALICE. The candy!
MARGE. Sure, Alice.
ALICE. The chocolate-covered peanuts!
MARGE. Sure, Alice. Here they are. Want some? (ALICE grabs box, hurls it upstage.)
ALICE. Don't you understand? They're doped!

MARGE (retreating). I heard you stopped drugs.
ALICE. Don't you understand?
MARGE. No.
ALICE. I'm tripping out!
MARGE. I better get your father.
ALICE (grabbing MARGE). No! He'll think I'm a dope fiend.
MARGE. Alice, please, let go of me. (They struggle, come close to bathroom door.) Please, Alice!
ALICE. Oh, God! They're in my hair! (Holding MARGE with one hand, ALICE hits her own head with other hand.)
MARGE. Alice!
ALICE. They're slimy! How can worms bite so hard? (Now ALICE is clutching MARGE in fear. MARGE manages to get bathroom door open, pushes ALICE inside, holds door closed.)
MARGE. Mr. Aberdeen!
ALICE (from bathroom). Help me! Oh, God, help me! They're eating me up!
MARGE. Mr. Aberdeen! Help! (FATHER and TIM yell from offstage, ALICE screams and moans, batters on door.)
FATHER (offstage). Who is it? Where are you?
TIM (offstage). Dad! In the basement!
MARGE. No! No! Alice's room!
ALICE (from bathroom). My eyes! They're

Act II   GO ASK ALICE   Page 81

    eating my eyes out!
MOTHER (offstage). Doug! Alice's room!
FATHER (offstage). What? (MARGE runs from
    room.)
MARGE (offstage). Here! Here!

(ALICE tumbles out of bathroom, her face, hair,
    and hands covered with blood.)

BLACKOUT

Scene Three

LIGHTS: BABBIE and GERTRUDE are sitting in a waiting room in a mental hospital. The table has been removed from [stage left] set and two wooden benches or a few chairs substituted. BABBIE wears old jeans, GERTRUDE wears an old, shapeless dress.)

GERTRUDE. Come on, Babbie, go buy me some Bugler.
BABBIE. I told you, the commissary isn't open yet. Besides, I have to wait for the bus to X-ray.
GERTRUDE. Then gimme a cigarette.
BABBIE. Buy your *own*.
GERTRUDE. Come on, buy me some Bugler. I'll roll you cigarettes.
BABBIE. I don't want any. They'll think it's a joint.
GERTRUDE. You smoke that stuff? Little girl like you? Thirteen, right? What's yer momma say about that?
BABBIE. She says smoke it out on the street.
GERTRUDE. Do you?
BABBIE. Come on, Gertrude, don't play your games.
GERTRUDE. Gimme a cigarette?

(Enter TOM. He is a patient, teen, dressed in pressed slacks, shirt and tie.)

TOM. How's it going, you two?

Act II   GO ASK ALICE   Page 83

GERTRUDE. Hi, Doc.
BABBIE. Here we go again.
TOM. I'm not a doctor, I'm just a patient like you.
GERTRUDE. You can't fool me, you're an intern.
TOM. Intern what?
GERTRUDE. International! (Big haw-haw laugh.)
BABBIE. Jesus, how many times do I have to
    listen to *that?*
TOM. Take it easy.
BABBIE. What are you doing here?
TOM. I'm on a break.
BABBIE. What's it like typing?
TOM. Not so bad. They don't expect much. The
    files are terrible. Half of it's filed under 'A'.
    Must have a patient who liked that letter. The
    important thing is that working in the office
    is gonna help me get out of this nut house.
BABBIE. Guess you're right.
TOM. Why don't you volunteer to work there, too?
BABBIE. I don't care where I am.
GERTRUDE. Buy me some Bugler, Tom?
TOM. Sure.
GERTRUDE. Good boy. Here's a half dollar.
    Jack Kennedy gave it to me.
TOM. Yeah? When?
GERTRUDE. When he stayed here. We used to
    play croquet together.
TOM. Who won?
GERTRUDE. I let 'em beat me. He was handsome.
    I divorced John Barrymore.

(Enter ALICE. She has bandages on her head,
    hands, wears jeans.)

TOM. Hi, Alice.

ALICE. Hi, hi, everybody. You look ready to
   leave the slammer, Tom.
TOM. I am, believe me. And you know the first
   thing I'm gonna do?
ALICE. Tell me.
TOM. I'm gonna buy me a combination bag. I'm
   gonna get so messed up, I'm gonna ——
ALICE. Okay, okay, I get it.
TOM. This time I'm gonna make sure I don't get
   busted.
ALICE. How's the office work?
TOM. I know some guys who were chem majors in
   college. They're waiting for me to get out.
BABBIE. How's the office work, Tom?
TOM. Listen, I am gonna really deal, I mean deal,
   and when I get a big bundle together, like
   ten or twenty grand, I'll do 'em all, man.
   I'm not afraid of smack. You just have to
   watch yourself. I know lots of guys who take
   it when they like and leave it alone when they
   like.
ALICE. Sure, sure. So what else is new, Tom?
TOM. What's with you two?
BABBIE. We're tired of listening to you talk about
   drugs all the time.
TOM. Square, right? A couple of squares.
BABBIE (sarcastically). Shoot me up, baby. Lemme
   fly low like a swallow.
TOM. Maybe when I buy Gertrude her Bugler I
   should get you a lollipop?
BABBIE. Would you? Please?
ALICE. Get me one, too? One of those big orange
   ones with a yellow stripe?
TOM. I've seen squares in my time, but you two
   got five right angles apiece.

Act II   GO ASK ALICE   Page 85

BABBIE. Buzz off.
TOM. You better believe that's just what I'm gonna do. (Exit TOM.)
GERTRUDE. You girls hurt his feelings.
BABBIE. I'm gonna take a walk. Alice, I'll be back in a few minutes.
ALICE. What if the X-ray bus comes?
BABBIE. I'll stay in the general area, don't worry. "General area?" I've been here too long. (Exit BABBIE.)
GERTRUDE. She a friend of yours?
ALICE. No, Gertrude, we're gonna kill each other tonight.
GERTRUDE. I was only *asking*.
ALICE. Gertrude, I like you, I really do. I wish you'd stop trying to make me dislike you.
GERTRUDE. I was only *asking*.
ALICE. You know Babbie and I are friends.
GERTRUDE. It's nice to be friends. Makes the time pass.
ALICE. Huh?

(Enter DOCTOR MILLER, a straightforward, pleasant woman psychiatrist.)

DR. MILLER. Hello, Alice, the nurse on the ward said I might find you here.
ALICE. Hello, Doctor Miller.
DR. MILLER. Well, Alice, I see your hair is growing back in nicely. Let's see your hands. Better, much better.
ALICE. I thought you were a psychiatrist.
DR. MILLER. So I am. Just looking, not doctoring.
ALICE. I didn't *mean* anything. I just wasn't sure.

GERTRUDE. She's a psychiatrist, all right.
DR. MILLER. Gertrude, maybe you'd let me talk to Alice?
GERTRUDE. Sure. Sorry.
DR. MILLER. That's all right. (DR. MILLER and ALICE turn so that they're facing downstage, their conversation carried away from upstage GERTRUDE.)
ALICE. Do you think they'll ever look the way they used to?
DR. MILLER. That's what I'm told. The nails, what I can see of them, are doing fine. I think you'll be all right physically.
ALICE. And mentally?
DR. MILLER. I'm sorry. I didn't mean it that way.
ALICE. That's okay. Doctor, I had a flashback a couple of days ago. It really scared me.
DR. MILLER. I'm sure it did. Did you report it?
ALICE. No.
DR. MILLER. You should have.
ALICE. It was a lot like when I tripped, when I did this to myself. I keep seeing these worms. Sometimes even when I'm okay I get real nervous when I see a fly or something, or I feel something on me. It's scary.
DR. MILLER. You probably internalized your feelings about your grandfather's death. I'm only sorry that in association with drugs it's produced these frightening nightmares, flashbacks and so forth.
ALICE. Someone told me if you have a bad flashback sleeping pills will at least knock you out so you don't have to go through it.
DR. MILLER. Let's talk about you.
ALICE. If it weren't for drugs I wouldn't be here.

Act II   GO ASK ALICE   Page 87

DR. MILLER. Alice, how do you think you'd feel on this date, today, if you'd never taken a drug?

ALICE. Fine! Terrific!

DR. MILLER. Are you sure? You remember telling me about the emotional difficulties you had before you ever took a single drug of any kind? (ALICE nods.) Alice, I'm not trying in any way to minimize your drug involvement. Please don't misunderstand me in that regard. I'm only suggesting that instead of concentrating all your energies on drugs being your one problem, that you take time to think about *yourself*.

ALICE. I do think about myself.

DR. MILLER. Do you?

ALICE. I told you I'm going to help people when I'm better. I'm going to devote my life to helping other people.

DR. MILLER. Other people? What about yourself, Alice? Don't you feel *you're* worth helping?

ALICE. I'm worth helping.

DR. MILLER. Do you really feel that way, or are you only saying it?

ALICE. No, I mean it. I have to help myself. I have to change. I can't be depressed all the time. I make myself depressed because I think negatively too much. I shouldn't do that.

DR. MILLER. What's wrong with thinking negatively?

ALICE. Well, look, you're a doctor, you're a psychiatrist. Kids on the Coast told me about this "I'm okay, you're okay" therapy. It keeps you from getting negative and down on yourself and everyone else.

DR. MILLER. But what if you don't *feel* okay? Is it bad to feel sad and miserable?

ALICE. If the whole world felt miserable, everything would come to a halt, no one would do anything.

DR. MILLER. We're not talking about the whole world. We're talking only about you. I want to know what's wrong with being miserable if that's the way you feel. (ALICE picks up Doctor's hand.) I'm not recommending that you spend the rest of your life feeling depressed. But you're very strict with yourself, Alice. You think you're supposed to live by some kind of rigid code, I *think*. I'm not sure. I want to talk to you some more. Try not to be so strict with yourself all the time. If you feel miserable and sorry for yourself go ahead and feel it. Don't deny it. (ALICE throws her arms around DOCTOR and cries.)

ALICE. I'm so *scared*. I feel so *awful!* (DOCTOR holds her gently. GERTRUDE jumps up.)

GERTRUDE. Look what you did! You made the little girl cry! Why did you do that?

DR. MILLER (waving GERTRUDE back with free hand). Sit down, Gertrude, everything is all right.

GERTRUDE. But the poor little girl.

ALICE. I'm okay, Gertrude. I'm sorry, Doctor.

DR. MILLER. Nothing to apologize about. Look, why don't we go to the commissary? I'll buy you something to drink.

ALICE. I'm supposed to wait for the X-ray bus.

DR. MILLER. I'll explain it to them.

ALICE. Well, okay. Thank you.

Act II GO ASK ALICE Page 89

(DR. MILLER and ALICE exit. After a few moments TOM reappears with BABBIE.)

TOM. Here's your tobacco. Hey, where'd Alice go?
GERTRUDE. With Doctor Miller.
TOM. Picking Alice's brains, eh? Those shrinks, always sticking their noses in someone else's business.
BABBIE. Into your business, too?
TOM. I just talk about sex to psychiatrists. That's all they want to hear, so that's what I talk about. I wouldn't mind doing that with Doctor Miller. Sex up the lady doctor.
BABBIE. Sex her up? You know what we are, dummy? Do you know? Huh?
TOM. What?
BABBIE. Nothing. Go sex yourself up.

BLACKOUT

GO ASK ALICE   Act II

Scene Four

LIGHTS: ALEXANDRIA is entering Alice's
    room carrying a large dish of peanut brittle.
    MOTHER and FATHER follow.)

ALEXANDRIA. Let's finish the party in here.
MOTHER. You're so insistent.
ALEXANDRIA. It's Alice's birthday, and she
    likes her room. So I think we should finish
    in here.
MOTHER. Well, all right.
FATHER. Alexandria, you're really getting bossy.
ALEXANDRIA. No, I'm not, I'm just telling you
    what to do. Now sit down, everybody.
    Where's Tim?
FATHER. He'll be along.
MOTHER. Shouldn't we get Alice?
ALEXANDRIA. Leave her alone right now. She's
    with her boy friend on the porch. (Peeks out
    window.) Maybe they're *kissing*.
MOTHER (laughing). What do we do at Alice's
    birthday party without Alice?
ALEXANDRIA. Nothing. (ALEXANDRIA plops
    on to bed, puts on headphones and tunes stereo
    radio.)
MOTHER. I'm confused.
FATHER. Me, too. Let's sit down and just relax.
    What do you think?
MOTHER. Doug, I think she's going to be all right.
FATHER. I think so, too. Society always refers
    to boys sowing wild oats. Maybe girls need to

do that, too, sometimes. Maybe that's what she was doing. (MOTHER rests her head on Father's shoulder.) She and Joel seem to have really hit it off.

MOTHER. I'm really proud of Alice. She's done so much these two months since she came back from the hospital.

FATHER. The way she practices the piano.

MOTHER. It's hard to believe she's going to be the featured soloist at the student recital.

FATHER. She loves practicing. It shows that you were right, dear, in making her take piano when she was little.

MOTHER. I suppose. But I can't go through that again with Alexandria.

FATHER. I can't really visualize Alexandria playing the piano, anyway.

MOTHER (laughing). No need for her to. Alice plays it so *well*.

FATHER. Alice did a fine job in summer school. B-plusses.

MOTHER. Grades aren't everything. But they ––

FATHER. –– *are* important. (Both laugh.)

MOTHER. And the phone is ringing a lot again.

FATHER. You and that phone. I think you measure the success of your children by the number of phone calls per week.

MOTHER. Doug, that's not true.

FATHER. I was only kidding.

MOTHER. But she *is* socializing again. And all the names are different: Fawn, Frank, Wally, Jess, Tess, Judy. They're *all* new friends.

FATHER. And *all* square, thank God.

MOTHER. Do you think we're trying to construct the perfect American daughter?

ALEXANDRIA (removing headphones). I'm bored.
FATHER. We'll send for the jester.
ALEXANDRIA. No. He doesn't please me. I'm
 having him flogged.
MOTHER. May I have another piece of Her
 Majesty's peanut brittle?
ALEXANDRIA. Take all you want. The slaves
 in the kitchen are preparing buckets.

(Enter TIM.)

TIM. I smelled peanut brittle in the kitchen.
ALEXANDRIA. You have to entertain me before
 you get a piece. (TIM tickles ALEXANDRIA;
 she laughs.) Okay, you can have some.
MOTHER. Hand me another piece, Tim.
 (ALEXANDRIA goes to window, sings.)
ALEXANDRIA. "Here comes the bride, all
 dressed in white." (She cups hands over her
 mouth, laughs.)
FATHER. Alexandria, don't you ever calm down?
MOTHER. That wasn't a very nice thing to do.
TIM. Alexandria is jealous of Alice.
ALEXANDRIA. I am not.
TIM. You are, too.
ALEXANDRIA. I am, too. (Giggles.)
TIM. I hear the boys on the football team like
 you, Alex. They use you for a tackle dummy.
ALEXANDRIA. Go back to your stink room.
 What are you making in there, germs for the
 next epidemic?
FATHER. Now, now. I don't want to referee
 today.
TIM. You don't have to, Dad. She won't last
 through the first round.

Act II   GO ASK ALICE   Page 93

ALEXANDRIA. What's that, One Punch?
FATHER. Okay, *okay!*
MOTHER. Stop it, you two.
TIM. We didn't mean anything. I like Alex. I
    like her a lot, even if she isn't all there.
ALEXANDRIA. Listen to him! He ——

(Enter ALICE and JOEL. ALICE wears white
    dress and sandals.)

ALICE. Listen to you! What was that song you
    were singing out the window?
ALEXANDRIA. Me?
JOEL (smiling). You.
ALEXANDRIA. How did I sound?
JOEL. Like an angel.
ALEXANDRIA (taking in group). Somebody who
    knows talent.
ALICE. How come everyone's in *here?*
MOTHER. Alexandria thought we should finish
    your party in your room.
FATHER (taking out envelope). Alice, here's
    your birthday present.
ALICE. Thank you.
ALEXANDRIA. Folding money. That's not as
    neat as what Tim and I gave her.
MOTHER. Alice, we're sorry your present wasn't
    delivered on time.
ALICE (taking out card and piece of paper). This
    is a picture of a leather coat.
FATHER. The coat was supposed to be here. It
    should be tomorrow or the next day.
ALICE. It's so beautiful! Thank you! Thank you!
    (She kisses both parents.)
JOEL. And I have this. (Gives her small jeweler's

box.)
ALEXANDRIA. I told you. "Here comes the ——".
TIM. Quiet.
ALEXANDRIA. Joel thinks I sing nice.
TIM. He feels sorry for you.
ALICE. It's a friendship ring! With little flowers all over it! Thank you, Joel! (Throws her arms around him, gives him quick kiss.)
ALEXANDRIA. Come on, Joel, have some of my peanut brittle. (Takes him by the hand.)
TIM. Alex has a crush on you, Joel.
ALEXANDRIA. I do not. I love him madly.
ALICE. Look at me. I get the ring one minute, I'm jilted the next.
ALEXANDRIA. You have to be aggressive, Alice. You can't stand around being a honey pot forever.
FATHER. A honey who? (TIM puts hand over Alexandria's mouth, she throws it off.)
ALEXANDRIA. Stop that! How's the peanut brittle?
JOEL. Delicious!
ALEXANDRIA. I make it better than Mom or Alice.
MOTHER. What makes you think so?
ALEXANDRIA. I heard you and Alice saying it. (Laughs.)
JOEL. Alice, I know you have to get up at six to practice for your recital.
ALICE. I wish I didn't.
JOEL. No, no, that's fine.
ALEXANDRIA. It is?
JOEL. I mean, it's not fine, but ——
ALEXANDRIA. It's not?
JOEL. Alexandria, you're getting me all mixed up.

(Everyone laughs.) I'll see you at seven tomorrow
   night, right?
ALICE. Right.
FATHER. Here, I'll drive you to your new place.
MOTHER. I'll come along, too, I've got that old
   toaster for you.
FATHER. Helen, you don't have to go on account
   of the toaster.
MOTHER. Of course I don't. But I want to see the
   kind of room Joel is living in.
TIM. Aw, Mother!
MOTHER. That's not what I mean. I'm sorry,
   Joel, I didn't say it the way I meant it. I'm
   not snooping. I just want to see if we can
   offer you an old rug, or chair or two, or
   whatever.
JOEL. Please come with. You, too, Tim.
ALEXANDRIA. I'm coming! I gonna take Joel
   away from Alice.
ALICE. Don't waste your time competing with
   your adult sister.
ALEXANDRIA. You're only *seventeen.*
ALICE. Your young adult sister.
ALEXANDRIA. Old *teen-ager.*
ALICE. I give. You talk circles around me.
FATHER (irritably). Come on, everyone, let's go.
   Alice, we'll be back later.
ALICE. Okay. Thanks for the wonderful birthday
   party, everybody!
ALL. You're welcome! (Group exits. ALICE sits
   down with her diary, reads aloud.)
ALICE. "Diaries are great when you're young.
   In fact, you saved my sanity a hundred,
   thousand, million times. But I think when a
   person gets older she should be able to discuss

her problems and thoughts with other people,
instead of just with another part of herself as
you have been to me. Don't you agree? I hope
so, for you are my dearest friend and I shall
thank you always for sharing my tears and
heartaches and my struggles and strifes, and
my joys and happinesses." (She then writes,
reading aloud.) It's all been good in its own
special way, I guess. See ya. (ALICE puts
pen down, puts diary back in box. As she
is closing the lid she suddenly shudders,
leaps up.) Flashback! (She runs to window,
screams.) Mother! Dad!

(ALICE rapidly exits and reenters with telephone,
dials and gets busy signal. She then throws
her hands over her face and screams. She runs
to the bed, rips off the bedspread, and as she
throws it over her, crosses rapidly to a corner
of the room. She backs into the corner,
touching both walls for reassurance, sinking
with spread wrapped around her up to the neck.
Then she buries her face in the spread and sobs.)

ALICE. Doctor Miller! Somebody! Our Father,
which art in heaven. Our Father, which art in
heaven. Somebody, please! Doctor Miller!

(ALICE runs to her bathroom, runs back out with
red bottle of pills, begins washing them down
with Coke left from party.)

ALICE. Doctor Miller! The worms! (ALICE hits
herself, runs back to bed and lies on it face
down, under the covers. Then she turns on
her side.) Sleep! Please! They'll go away if

Act II   GO ASK ALICE   Page 97

I *sleep!* (ALICE sobs. There is slow dimming of lights to establish passage of time as setting of sun. ALICE turns on her back and throws one arm out beyond the bed, in exactly the same position that ended the opening scene of the play after she took the sleeping pill. Sound of front door. Voices are heard.)

(MOTHER opens door of Alice's room, stands in doorway with FATHER.)

MOTHER. Joel has a nice room, dear.
FATHER. Did we have to spend so long in it? (FATHER enters the room, goes to Alice's bed, whispers to MOTHER.) She fell asleep with her clothes on. I'll just cover her. (He touches ALICE.) Alice! Alice! My God!
MOTHER. Douglas! What!
FATHER. She's cold! Cold! (MOTHER runs to Alice's bed.)
MOTHER. Doug, she's not breathing! Douglas!
FATHER. She's cold! She's dead!
MOTHER. Alice! No! Let me die!

(MOTHER, weeping, embraces Alice's dead body. ALEXANDRIA and TIM race into room and stop, staring at spectacle. FATHER spots red pill bottle on floor, picks bottle up, in anguish hurls it back at floor. TIM presses Alexandria's face to his chest, so she can't see. Actors freeze for a count of two, quick blackout.)

THE END

SYNOPSIS OF SCENES

ACT ONE

Scene One: Alice's room. Summer.

Scene Two: Same. A few days later.

Scene Three: Same. Three months later.

ACT TWO

Scene One: Simultaneous action in Alice's room and back room of store in San Francisco. Less than three months later.

Scene Two: Alice's room. Four months later.

Scene Three: Waiting room in mental hospital. Two months later.

Scene Four: Alice's room. Three months later.

NOTES ON CHARACTERS, PROPERTIES AND COSTUMES

SETTING: A simple split set is utilized, the division between playing areas made with a cutaway flat or other convention. Alice's room is stage right, about two-thirds of the stage. It has a twin bed, small desk, a number of cushions or pillows on floor, area rug, a toy chest from her childhood, other typical appointments such as bean-bag chair, hard varnished chairs, a stereo and television, a bookcase crammed to the last inch. The room has its own bathroom, one door, a window. It is usually in a state of disorder, with magazines, etc. scattered about. Stage left is little more than a smaller room with an archway upstage. This area is used in Act Two, Scenes One and Three.

PERSONAL:
Act One, Scene One:

MOTHER: Dust mop, nightgown for Alice.
SAMUEL: Casual clothes, probably jeans and shirt.
BETH: Casual clothes, probably jeans and blouse. Purse.
FATHER: Bag or box of chocolate-covered peanuts; red bottle with sleeping pills in it.
ALICE: Jeans and blouse; toward end of scene she dons another blouse and puts floor-length nightgown over it. Small flashlight.

Act One, Scene Two:

ALICE: Jeans, a different blouse than the one she

had on in Scene One.
CHRIS, JOE, BILL, JAN and GLORIA: Casual clothes, probably jeans, blouses and shirts. The girls carry purses.
GLORIA: Bottles of Coke.

Act One, Scene Three:

ALICE: Vest or neck scarf over same clothes as Scene Two. Vial of pills from Chris's purse.
CHRIS: Different blouse from Scene Two. Two cups of coffee.
ALEXANDRIA and TIM: Pajamas.

Act Two, Scene One:

MOTHER: Flat package with plastic drop cloth inside; dust mop; telephone on extension.
FATHER: Fat manila folder; airline schedules.
FREDDIE: Leather jacket, heavy botts.
ALICE: Pieces of red velvet cloth; strongbox with diary in it; box of dried cereal.
SHEILA: Elegantly dressed, wears dark glasses.
CHRIS: Telephone on extension.

Act Two, Scene Two:

MOTHER: Tape measure, pencil.
FATHER: Alexandria's report card.
GEORGE: Very conservatively dressed — possibly a suit and tie.
JOEL: Book.

Act Two, Scene Three:

BABBIE: Old jeans.

GERTRUDE: Wears old, shapeless dress; half a dollar.
TOM: Wears pressed slacks, shirt and tie; bag of tobacco.
ALICE: Jeans, bandages on head and hands.
DR. MILLER: Wears dress or pants suit.

Act Two, Scene Four:

ALEXANDRIA: Large dish of peanut brittle.
ALICE: White dress, sandals; telephone on extension; Coke; bottle of red pills.
FATHER: Envelope with money, card and piece of paper in it.
JOEL: Small jewelers box with ring in it.

DIRECTOR'S NOTES

DIRECTOR'S NOTES

DIRECTOR'S NOTES

DIRECTOR'S NOTES

DIRECTOR'S NOTES

DIRECTOR'S NOTES

DIRECTOR'S NOTES

DIRECTOR'S NOTES

DIRECTOR'S NOTES

DIRECTOR'S NOTES

DIRECTOR'S NOTES